Blooming in Full Color

a novel by
EUGENIE
DAVIDSEN

◆ FriesenPress

Suite 300 - 990 Fort St
Victoria, BC, V8V 3K2
Canada

www.friesenpress.com

Copyright © 2016 by Eugenie Davidsen
First Edition — 2016

Cover Illustrations:
– Front cover, hibiscus grandiflorus and blue-winged yellow Warbler. courtesy of Swallowtail Garden Seeds (1826-1838), sourced from flickr.com
– Front cover, poppy diagram illustration originally published by A.W. Mumford, Chicago, 1900, Sourced from the Internet Archive Book Images profile on Flickr.com
– Back cover, poppy illustration originally published by Klincksieck, Paris, 1896, sourced from the Internet Archive Book Images profile on Flickr.com

Interior poppy graphics sourced from freepik.com

All rights reserved.

No part of this publication may be reproduced in any form, or by any means, electronic or mechanical, including photocopying, recording, or any information browsing, storage, or retrieval system, without permission in writing from FriesenPress.

ISBN
978-1-4602-8941-9 (Hardcover)
978-1-4602-8942-6 (Paperback)
978-1-4602-8943-3 (eBook)

1. FICTION, CHRISTIAN, ROMANCE

Distributed to the trade by The Ingram Book Company

"This book is dedicated to my readers.
Your faith, trust and encouragement has been my inspiration."

TABLE OF CONTENTS

Chapter 1
Will You Be My Daddy?. 1

Chapter 2
Blooming 5

Chapter 3
Caring – Cindy 9

Chapter 4
Anna. 12

Chapter 5
Meaghan's Debut 14

Chapter 6
Luc – Internal Struggle. 19

Chapter 7
Sara the Caregiver 22

Chapter 8
Luc – Choices 25

Chapter 9
Marty. 28

Chapter 10
Luc and Sara 31

Chapter 11
Frog Slippers 34

Chapter 12
Sara Remembering. 38

Chapter 13
Marty Trouble 43

Chapter 14
Date Night 45

Chapter 15
Mario's Bar and Grill 48

Chapter 16
Baby News 55

Chapter 17
Popeye's Pancakes 58

Chapter 18
Meaghan 68

Chapter 19
Hunting for Treasure 71

Chapter 20
More Marty Trouble 77

Chapter 21
Dad or No Dad 80

Chapter 22
Leaving Vancouver 83

Chapter 23
Anna and Silk 86

Chapter 24
Luc and Lisa 90

Chapter 25
A Real Dad 94

Chapter 26
Three Months Later –
Falling In Love 96

Chapter 27
What's In a Name? 99

Chapter 28
Marty Sings the Blues 102

Chapter 29
I Do I Do I Do 105

Chapter 1

WILL YOU BE MY DADDY?

"Are you going to be my daddy?" three-year-old Cohen asked, tilting his head back and looking way up at his tall friend.

Luc's mind was buzzing! *What does a guy say to a three-year-old who's looking for only one answer?* With eyes squinted, he looked down at his young buddy. After what seemed like a very long time, Luc stooped down onto his haunches and returned Cohen's direct gaze – he was at a loss for words, so he said nothing. His eyes filled with compassion.

Luc and his mother Sara, who was Tara and Cohen's caregiver, were on an adventure to Marine World at the Vancouver Aquarium.

Finally Luc raised his glance from Cohen to look up at his mother. Their eyes met, she had been listening carefully – hardly daring to breathe. Luc stood up and the foursome began slowly walking. A few steps later, Cohen asked once again.

"Luc, will you be my daddy? *Puleeese?*" Then in the same breath, he went on to exclaim in a shrill, excited voice, "Oh look at it, Luc, it's a *ginormous* stingray."

At that precise moment Cohen had spied a massive languid stingray floating in the water on the other side of the glass enclosure. The stingray's huge bulgy eyes were glued onto a group of people surrounding it and thankfully Cohen had lost his train of thought about the previous question.

"Oh look at it! Is it really a stingray? Where's his mouth? I can't even see his nose! Where's his nose?" Cohen asked, words tumbling out of his mouth. He was overjoyed.

"It sure is a ginormous stingray, Cohen," Luc replied mussing Cohen's black hair with his huge hand.

"What's a stingray?" Tara asked, joining in the conversation.

"I think a stingray belongs to the shark family, if I remember right," Luc replied.

"This one is certainly a fine, giant specimen. His mouth and nose are on his underbelly.

Maybe we'll get to see them if he swims higher up in the water."

"How come he's so big?" Cohen asked, becoming totally sidetracked with the stingray.

"My guess is that he eats a lot of food, whatever that is. When we get back to our hotel we'll have to look it up online and find out what he eats," Luc informed the little group.

"Oh look, his color is changing. That's pretty amazing! Can you change your color, Cohen? How about you Tara, does your blonde hair change to red, or blue?" Luc asked.

Tara looked at Luc and started laughing. "You're silly," she exclaimed. "Of course I can't change my hair color. I'm not a fish, I'm a person. People can't change colors."

Cohen lost his interest in the giant stingray and ran ahead to see what was in the next window.

"Just a minute, Cohen," Luc warned, "Let's wait for Sara." Sara had slipped over to the ticketing desk to purchase admission passes for the foursome.

"What's this?" Cohen asked, pointing to another giant sea creature.

Sara caught up to the group and exchanged a "look" with Luc. Both of them seemed to simultaneously breathe a sigh of relief at the forgotten "Dad" question.

"I'll try and answer this one." Sara informed her son. "You take a break. I'm sure there will be more questions to answer as the day goes along!"

Cohen wants me to be his daddy, Luc thought. *Poor little guy. I wonder what that's all about. I better have a talk with Meaghan first chance and find out what's going on!"*

Meaghan, the children's mother had been hired by the Enlighten Weight Loss Company and in turn had hired Luc's mother Sara as their caregiver. The first leg of their Enlighten journey had begun in Vancouver. Luc's occupation as a commercial airline pilot enabled him to fly to Vancouver and be able to spend his days off with his mother and her charges.

Sara, Tara, Cohen and Luc spent the morning happily viewing the sea creature exhibits. As they neared the exit sign they noticed they were right in time for a trained dolphin show. They found seats and settled down to watch the amazing creatures perform. After the show Cohen spied a foursome of penguins cutely dressed in miniature tuxedoes and acting as doormen.

It was past lunch time and everyone was hungry so when they spied an empty table and four chairs in the food court, they quickly plopped themselves down. Luc went to the counter and ordered four fish and chip meals.

"I wonder which fish we're eating," Cohen asked, stuffing his mouth full of food. He looked up at Sara and then Luc, his eyes huge and innocent.

The question took Sara and Luc by surprise and they looked at each other for enlightenment.

"That's a good question, Cohen." Luc replied with a twinkle in his eyes. "When we're finished eating, we'll go and ask the man we bought it from. Maybe it's the dolphin we saw jumping through the hoop, or maybe it's the stingray with the big bulgy eyes that was watching us so closely."

"*No way!*" Tara stated her eyes wide, "They wouldn't let us eat their famous fish!" She thought for a moment and then added, "Maybe the ones we get to eat are the ones that won't listen to the trainers; I think we get to eat the bad ones."

Luc looked at Sara and chuckled, "You know what Tara? I think you're probably right. What else could they do with the bad ones?"

Chapter 2

BLOOMING

Meaghan stepped inside her beautiful, luxuriant hotel suite and let out a "Hello, I'm home." No answer. *I wonder where everyone is.* She thought, setting her shoulder bag down beside the kitchen island and absent mindedly giving it a little nudge under the stool with her toe.

Wandering into her bedroom, she leisurely began changing from her work clothes into casual attire.

Her mind drifted over the last few weeks of her life and she marvelled at the changes that had occurred.

No longer was she the sole caretaker of her two precious children, Tara and Cohen. Meaghan felt that it seemed like the children were thriving in their new living arrangement. Sara was doing a great job as their nanny, and having the added attention of Sara's son Luc in their lives was definitely a bonus! She believed the children were becoming more self confident, less needy. Their shyness was disappearing while at the same time they were having a blast, taking part in some of the big city adventures that were available to them. Cohen and Tara were learning how to form relationships with other people. *Such a valuable life lesson,* Meaghan thought.

Overall, Meaghan was happy and content, confident that she had made the right decision to go on the Canadian tour for the Enlighten Weight Loss Program. The agenda was certainly challenging her to be the best she could be. Five days a week her daily routine consisted of rising before dawn, heading downstairs to the hotel swimming pool to partake in swimming laps, and then over to the gym to work out on the resistance machines, or occasionally pumping iron. After an hour of exercising she would head off to the shower and then the makeup department.

On normal business days, Meaghan would apply her own makeup, but on photo shoot days an artist would come in and "do" her up professionally. Next on her daily agenda was the "hair" studio.

Meaghan's mind returned to the word "normal" and she chuckled. *There is nothing normal about my life right now! I don't know how it happened, or why, but here I am on this amazing adventure and I'm having a wonderful time. I'm not lonely anymore. I have lots of great, quality time with my kids and tons of support from Sara and the Enlighten team and it's all so much fun. Thank you, Lord,* she thought, as she lifted her arms in the air and spread them out as if embracing God. *Life is good.*

Tomorrow was the Big Day. Meaghan would be introduced publicly to the whole country. A huge festival, planned by the Administrators of the Enlighten Organization at the Vancouver Centennial Convention Centre was planned at ten o'clock in the morning. Invitations had been sent out to every television station in the city. City dignitaries as well as provincial were all invited. Business owners and corporate sponsors were on the guest list as well. Meaghan knew there would be over three hundred people in attendance and felt very humbled.

Suddenly, Meaghan's thoughts were interrupted by voices on the other side of the door. Quickly jumping up, with a happy smile on her face, she rushed to open the door and see what all the noise was about.

"Mom, you're home!" Tara squealed as she and Cohen both came barrelling at her with arms outstretched. Meaghan knelt down, and braced herself with eyes closed. She wrapped her arms around her two beautiful children as they ploughed into her. She gave them a long tight squeeze.

Suddenly, Cohen stepped back and asked, "Mommy, do we have a daddy? I need to know if we have one, cause I saw one on TV and why don't I have a daddy?" His big blue eyes searched his mother's surprised face.

"Well Cohen, you do have a daddy. But he's not here. Can we talk about this later?" Meaghan answered.

"I asked Luc if he could be my daddy," Cohen solemnly told his mother.

Meaghan glanced over at Tara and then raised her glance to look up at Luc, who was standing in the doorway with Sara.

"I'm so sorry Luc, he doesn't understand," Meaghan responded.

"Not to worry, Meaghan. Cohen, if I were to have a little boy I would want him to be exactly like you," Luc said stroking Cohen's hair with his big hand.

"Okay," Meaghan said. "Why don't you two hang up your hoodies and go wash your hands? I'll see if I can find you something yummy for a snack."

The children hurried away and Meaghan apologized once again for Cohen's question and Luc for a second time informed her that it was not a big deal, "Just forget about it."

Somewhere in the distance Meaghan could hear her cell phone ringing and her eyes darted around the room looking for her shoulder bag! "Where did I put my bag?" She asked under her breath.

"Is this what you're looking for?" Luc asked picking up the handbag partially hidden under the kitchen stool.

"Yes, thanks Luc," Meaghan replied, rewarding him with a smile. "Excuse me for a minute," she continued as she rummaged in the bag for her cell phone.

"Of course, madam" Luc responded with a slight bow, perched himself onto the stool and picked up the morning newspaper.

"Hallo," Meaghan spoke into the phone.

"Hello, Meaghan, my name is Cindy Baldman Fresson. You don't know me but I'm Anna Baldman's daughter and my dad told me you took Mom's place as Enlighten Weight Loss Representative when Mom got cancer. I just wanted to give you an update on her condition."

"Oh, of course, Cindy, I remember your mother. How nice of you to call. Please tell me, how is your mother doing?"

"Mom is doing okay. The worst is over, I think. She underwent a double mastectomy and came through it without any complications so far. She's a tough little lady and is determined to pull through this" Cindy replied.

"Oh, that's so good to hear, thanks again for calling to tell me. I will pass this news on to Sara. Did you know that Sara and I were the ones who originally chose your mother to be the Enlighten Weight Loss Rep. for Canada?"

"You know Meaghan, I'm not sure if I knew that. So much has happened in the last year. But thank you for doing that for my mom. In my mind she's always been a highly talented outstanding person and deserves the best. How is the tour with Enlighten going?"

"Well we're just starting in Vancouver. It's all still very new to me, but I'm incredibly excited and can't wait to see what comes next. I feel very much like Cinderella must have felt, not quite fitting in at the ball!" Meaghan replied.

"I'm sure you'll do just fine, Meaghan," Cindy said. "Dad told me that Mom spoke very highly of you and was pleased that you were chosen to take her place."

"Thank you for passing that on, Cindy. I'm glad to hear that your mom is doing so well. Sara will be very pleased to hear this as well. We will certainly be praying for her complete recovery."

"You're welcome Meaghan. I wish you all the best with your tour. I'll tell Mom that I spoke to you and that you're praying for her. It's been good to have this chat with you, bye for now Meaghan."

"Bye Cindy, and thanks again." Meaghan said, hanging up the phone. She glanced over at Luc.

Chapter 3
CARING – CINDY

Cindy had a peaceful smile on her face as she hung up the phone. *Meaghan sounds like a very nice person,* she thought. Then glancing at the clock above the kitchen table she had a slight panic attack as she realized it was time to get to work. Gathering up her job paraphernalia she carried it out to her white sports utility vehicle and hoisted it inside.

After travelling a couple of blocks she thought, *the traffic is crazy this morning, what's going on?* Work for Cindy was a twelve-hour shift at the University Memorial Hospital in Swift Current, Saskatchewan, as a registered nurse. Cindy slowly drove along, her mind wandering to her mother's health condition.

Poor mom, she's been forced to give up a lot because of this rotten breast cancer.

Becoming Enlighten Weight Loss Representative for Canada was a big deal and Mom deserved it. But Cindy knew in her heart that her mom and dad were right. Mom's health had to come before any professional commitments.

Mom's gone through rounds of radiation. I sure hope it works.

Cindy's dream of becoming a nurse began straight out of kindergarten. She remembered her mother, always encouraging and telling her that she'd been born with an all-consuming compassion for anything hurting – two legged or four legged. Thinking back to her childhood, Cindy remembered her parents, Anna and Silk being very concerned many times when she would come home from school wailing over an injustice that had happened and someone had gotten hurt. Or from time to time she would come across an injured stray animal. She recalls at all times stopping to try and help, even though her parents warned her about getting close to a hurting animal.

Stopping for a red light one unusual incident came to Cindy's mind. A little boy that Cindy didn't know was sitting dejectedly on a street curb, as she was walking home from school. He seemed to be about five or six years old. It was the day after Cindy's eighth Birthday. The little boy was trying to hide a huge purple and red bruise on the side of his face with his tiny hand.

Cindy spotted the bruise and asked, "What happened to you?" her cerulean blue eyes filled with compassion as she knelt down in front of the poor child.

The little boy didn't know what to say. He looked intently into Cindy's eyes. After a few seconds the boy looked down and said quietly, "I fell."

Cindy wasn't sure if she believed him or not, but she asked, "Where do you live, do you want me to walk you home?"

The little boy replied immediately, "No – no, its okay. My dad is home, but he's busy right now. He told me to come back later."

Cindy remembered feeling so bad for the little boy. Her heart was breaking – but what could she do? And then she asked him, "Do you want to come home with me and have some supper?"

She felt that he really wanted to come with her but said, "No, I better wait here."

Cindy hurried home and shared the story about the little boy with her mother.

"Do you think someone hurt him, Mom?" she remembered bawling.

Cindy's mother listened compassionately and then said, "It could be Cindy, I don't know. Why don't we pray for him right now?" and they did.

The traffic light turned green and Cindy's mind snapped back to the present. As she started driving, Cindy began thinking of her husband, Hal. He would be home on the weekend, only two days away. Hal's profession was a mining engineer working with the Saskatchewan Natural Gas Company. His job required him to be away most weekdays, assessing new mine sites and reclaiming old ones, working with specialist software to support planning programs, overseeing major construction projects and ensuring that operations ran smoothly. He planned the transition from surface to underground mining operations, managing monthly budgets and keeping detailed records. The details of Hal's job description never ended, but he loved it.

One thing he made sure of when he came home on weekends and that was, he gave his full attention to his wonderful wife and their children. Cindy's mind wandered to their three beautiful babies, Sophie, now seven, she was so beautiful inside and out. Little Levi, he was small for his age, but his heart was big enough to be ten-years-old. And then there was the youngest David, now three. David's love language was definitely touching. He loved his parents and grandparents to touch his hands or his face or his feet.

The children brought a smile to Cindy's face.

Sometimes Hal's weekends consisted of a quick one day visit, but that was very rare and most weekends he made a point of being home from Friday afternoon to Monday morning. As much as he enjoyed his work, he deeply loved his wife and babies and didn't want to miss the milestones in their lives.

He had seen too many of his workmates marriages end up in a divorce. It wasn't easy being married and living apart. Temptations came along every day. His wise mother's warnings about marriage and commitment requiring time and energy and communication always hovered in the back of his mind and Hal felt that nothing worthwhile should be taken for granted, especially your marriage and family!

Chapter 4
ANNA

Anna was trembling with excitement! She was due to be released from the Oncology ward this morning. After undergoing a double mastectomy and receiving a binary breast implant she felt that every fibre of her body was hurting and protesting. It was going to be great to leave this place and be able to relax in more comfortable surroundings.

Anna knew without a doubt that her husband Silk would be a wonderful caregiver. He had an amazing knack of being everywhere at once and sensing her needs even before she knew what they were.

Anna vaguely remembers her daughter Cindy coming to the hospital at least once to visit her, but because of the heavy medication, her memories were very unclear. She distantly remembers hearing the phone constantly ringing – or so it seemed to her. Silk told her that everybody was concerned about her and calling to find out her condition.

Anna thought, *only You know my condition God. I strongly feel that I'm going to overcome this disease and I know that feeling must come from You, God.*

I'm going to trust that this is the end of my cancer, in Jesus, Your precious son's name I say,

Thank You, Amen.

Anna moved slightly in her bed trying to get more comfortable, but stopped quickly. It hurt. The medical team had decided to radically remove both of Anna's breasts, even though only one side had been affected with the cancer. They felt the possibility of the cancer recurring was very likely – so with Anna's consent they took the added precaution of removing both.

Anna also chose to have surgical implants put in place after the surgery. Her doctor warned her that the healing period would be longer with the implants, but she certainly didn't want to go through surgery again so in her mind it was the only option.

The morning nurse had propped Anna up in her bed with a mound of soft comfy pillows. Anna grabbed the television remote control and began channel surfing.

Nothing caught her attention. She hit the mute button, laid her head back on the pillows and relaxed. Soon she was fast asleep.

★★★

Silk silently slid a key into the front door of his borrowed accommodations and gave it a twist.

Holding the door open with his foot, he wedged his body through the opening. He was carrying two big brown paper bags overflowing with groceries. Quickly setting them on the kitchen counter, Silk walked quietly into the master bedroom. He was excited, Anna was coming home today; he needed to make the room ready for her.

Poor sweet Anna, he thought. *She's been through so much, what a trouper. She never complains or makes demands. She seems to have accepted her situation, like it's just another adventure and when it's over she'll be a stronger person. What can't kill you makes you stronger, right? That's Anna's motto. I have to admire her for that. I might not be so gracious, if this infliction was on me. Thank You God, for the grace you have given Anna to get through this ordeal.*

Chapter 5
MEAGHAN'S DEBUT

Meaghan was ready to face the world! The rigorous exercise routine and punctilious food program she was adhering to was paying off big time and she felt exhilarated.

Her body and mind had been whipped into shape for her unveiling. She felt healthy and strong and more in control of her life than she had for many years, giving her a great deal of much needed self-confidence and poise – she knew she had never experienced this before.

"Meaghan." She heard her name being called. The television crew was in the process of setting up for the Enlighten Weight Loss unveiling of which Meaghan was the star. The short television segment would be all about her and the promotion of the Enlighten Weight Loss Program. She would be required to be in every shot along with local dignitaries and the "Program" people.

Meaghan's introduction to the world was set up as a gala event, even though it was being filmed at ten o'clock in the morning. It would be aired on this evening's television broadcast.

The star looked magnificent in a shimmering silver knee length dress made of fine, lightweight organza, which actually appeared to glow in several deep rich colors that it picked up from the overhead lights. The snug fitting bodice featured a sweetheart neckline with tiny appliquéd pearls adorning the décolletage.

Meaghan's expertly applied makeup was perfection. For the premiere, her long shimmering black hair had been braided into several long thick braids which were then gently twisted around her head, in Grecian goddess style. For the finishing touch, miniature violet orchids were pinned in place throughout the braids. The look was breathtaking!

Meaghan couldn't help herself and let out a silent prayer. *God thank You so much for this life that You have led me into. I am so overjoyed to be where I am right now. My children are happy. I thank You that we are all healthy. Thank You for Sara and Luc and all the people involved with the Enlighten Group, Lord. I ask for Your healing touch on Anna. You are awesome, God. In Jesus Christ's name I say thank You, thank You, thank You, a thousand thank Yous. Amen.*

"Ms. Marshall." Meaghan was being paged on the intercom, "We need you front stage, right now, please." The producer of the event was ready to put people in their places; the debut was about to begin.

Meaghan didn't have a prepared script, which left her feeling somewhat uncertain. She was hoping she wouldn't trip over her words in her nervousness. She once again sent up a quick prayer, *God please let the words that come out of my mouth be honourable to You as well as to this wonderful company that is giving me this golden opportunity. In Jesus name I pray. Amen.*

The team quickly assembled the guests and the cameras started rolling. Meaghan's duty was to mingle among the guests, answering any questions they might have regarding the upcoming tour, the Enlighten Weight Loss Program and/or questions about her personal life.

The first guest Meaghan was introduced to and chatted with was Vancouver's honourable Mayor Rabild Lussan. During the interview Meaghan couldn't help but notice how very thin Mr. Lussan was, and nervously thought, *"He sure doesn't need the Enlighten Weight Loss Program."* All in all Meaghan believed the interview with the mayor went well. To the best of her ability

Meaghan explained to him exactly what the Enlighten Program was all about and the benefits this program would add to his city. She felt sure that the television crew had captured it all.

Next, Meaghan moved on to meet BC Premier Peter Cummingworth. Peter congratulated Meaghan on her position as the weight loss representative for Canada and then she seemed to lose his attention. It appeared to Meaghan that he fell into a trance. Meaghan tried her best to make small talk, sharing with him what the Enlighten Program was all about and regaling her experiences with the program so far. She gave him every opportunity to ask questions, which were not forthcoming. Meaghan filled in the silence with a few questions directed towards him and his role as premier. The head of government however could not be roused out of his deep thoughts and Meaghan wasn't sure what to do.

Looking around for reprieve Meaghan spied Cassandra out of the corner of her eye. Cassandra was the Enlighten Weight Loss president and Meaghan raised her hand in a casual wave and mouthed the word, *Help!* Cassandra acknowledged the wave and made her way over to join Meaghan and the premier.

"It was a pleasure meeting you, Mr. Cummingworth," Meaghan said, firmly shaking his hand.

"Likewise, Ms. Umm," he replied. "Perhaps we can get together for a glass of wine sometime?"

"Marshall, my name is Marshall" Meaghan answered. The cameraman switched off the camera and Meaghan and Cassandra moved away.

"Come with me, I have someone I *really* want you to meet, Meaghan." Cassandra told her.

The two women made their way through the crowd towards a tiny middle-aged Asian lady that Meaghan recognized as Serena Chu from the daily talk show, Good Morning Vancouver.

Serena pounced on Meaghan with an endless list of questions about the Enlighten Program. Then she asked Meaghan about her personal life, including her hopes and dreams.

Meaghan's head began to spin. She had enjoyed sharing her perspective on her new weight loss position and the purpose behind it, but she was getting uneasy with the questions. Serena's interview was starting to get extremely personal and she was not letting up. Meaghan wanted it to stop, so she once again signalled Cassandra, who was standing just a few feet away.

Cassandra expertly wrapped up Ms. Chu's questioning by thanking her for the lovely interview and saying, "We must move along!" Embracing Serena Chu, she planted a kiss first on one cheek and then the other and then with big smiles they bid adieu to Serena and Cassandra scuttled Meaghan off to the beverage buffet.

"Isn't this a great gathering, Meaghan?" Cassandra gushed. "You're doing great, aren't you? It's not too difficult for you? I know it's your first public appearance as spokesperson and it can be frightening, surrounded by all these officials and cameras stuck in your face, but remember they all wish you well and they will become your biggest fans. Everyone here is just doing their job. Take a deep breath and put on that glorious smile. Oh, here comes Rhiana Redford. She's one of our main sponsors in the clothing line."

Meaghan couldn't suppress a little giggle and asked, "Become my fans, Cassandra?"

Rhiana walked right up to Meaghan and Cassandra, extending a perfectly manicured right hand as she approached. The three ladies all shook hands, while Cassandra made the introductions.

Meaghan's first thought about Rhiana was that she had a mass of red hair. Long tresses of burgandy-red curls hung down Rhiana's back and shoulders. Meaghan guessed her to be in her late thirties. *Rhiana looks perfect*, Meaghan thought, *"her hair, her makeup, her body language, her apparel. She has the poise and confidence roles down to a T! I wonder if I'll ever get that much self-confidence.*

Rhiana fired questions at Meaghan and Meaghan fired the answers right back. The two ladies experienced a natural rapport and Meaghan relaxed to the point of forgetting she was being filmed and started having fun. She let out a deep belly laugh when Rhiana questioned her about Cohen and Tara. Although the questions were personal, Meaghan didn't feel threatened in any way. Rhiana was enjoying the stories about Cohen's latest antics and her interview took on the form of getting across to the public that Meaghan was a real person with children and a normal life when she wasn't on the spotlight with the Enlighten Program.

Rhiana was captivated by Meaghan's candour and suggested she would like to meet with her again sometime, off camera to continue their conversation. "I feel like we have a lot in common, maybe we can become friends."

"I would like that," Meaghan replied. "I'd love for you to meet my children, and hear more about your family."

"Okay," Rhiana said. "I'll call you and we can set up a date. Until then, take care of yourself, Meaghan." Cassandra hurried over, gave Rhiana a big smile and Meaghan was hustled off to her next interview.

After the interview with Rhiana, Meghan decided to relax and let her guard down a little. She knew there must be some very nice, normal people here and she really wanted to just be herself and enjoy the moment. So throughout the rest of the morning, and the next set of the interviews, she tried to remember what Cassandra was always telling her: "Meaghan, you are important too!"

Somehow Meaghan had never felt special, she was just a person. Her parents were wonderful hard working people that had taught her that it wasn't about her. Her role on this earth was to be helpful and make life easier for her family. Meaghan found it hard to switch to the mindset of putting herself first and not only first but in the spotlight – the centre of attention.

However Meaghan resolved that she would try her best.

Chapter 6
LUC – INTERNAL STRUGGLE

Luc was nearing his hotel room when he heard his cell phone ringing. He had changed the sound of the ring to "wildlife sounds" and he could hear a Loon call – it took him a few seconds to realize what was going on. Quickly frisking his pockets for his phone, he found the culprit and pushed the on button. *Hope I'm not too late!*

"Hello, hello!" he shouted into the mouthpiece.

"Hey Luc," a slight pause and then, "How are you?" Luc heard a silky female voice, on the other end of the line.

"I'm fine, who is this?" He hesitated and then realizing who it was asked, "Lisa, is that you?"

"Yes it's me, Luc. I've been thinking about you – a lot, and I would like to get together, we need to discuss something important. Are you up for that?"

"Yes, of course, but where are you? I'm in Vancouver." Luc informed his ex-girlfriend.

"I'm in Saskatoon." Lisa replied.

"Well, can we make it in a couple of days then? I'll be flying into Saskatoon on Tuesday for an overnighter. Could we meet up Tuesday evening?"

"Of course Luc, that will be all right, Tuesday evening at the Red Lion Bar and Grill – about eight o'clock?"

"Okay, sure, that's fine. Oh, but Lisa, what about the baby? Do you still have the baby?" Luc asked.

"That's what I want to talk to you about, Luc. I've come to the conclusion that you're a good man. There's not many like you around, and I miss you!"

Luc pulled the phone away from his ear and studied it for a couple of seconds, as if searching for clarification on Lisa's change of attitude. With a puzzled look on his face, he thought, *what is going on?* Then returning the phone to his ear he replied, "Okay, Tuesday at eight o'clock it is, at the Red Lion Grill. Thanks for calling and take care of yourself."

Luc hoped his voice sounded more sincere than he felt. He clicked off the phone connection and his thoughts wandered back over the past few weeks. *Lisa and I have a casual relationship – it becomes very physical – neither of us takes the proper precautions and – Lisa finds herself pregnant. I pursue Lisa for weeks and she doesn't respond. Now, when I've finally made the decision to leave it alone and move on, she decides to call and wants us to get together and take up where we left off. That's very interesting. I wonder what's on that little lady's agenda.*

Luc was curious about his baby though. *Lisa hadn't given away anything about the baby,* he thought. *I wonder if she's already aborted it. What is that woman up to?*

***

Inside Luc's hotel room he undressed and stepped into a steaming hot shower. His mind was traveling at high speed dreaming up all kinds of scenarios that might happen with this new development.

I can't see myself with Lisa anymore, not since I've met Meaghan. Meaghan's a great friend to me, we have so much in common, and if all goes well, I'm hoping our friendship will develop into something more serious! I am really attracted to her. I have nothing but respect and admiration for that woman. She's been raising those two adorable children on her own and doing an excellent job.

Meaghan's positive attitude challenged Luc to step up to his responsibilities. *She is a determined, focused person, moving forward and only thinking and wanting the best life for her and her children. I need to be more like that and be there for my child! I wonder if it's a boy or a girl.* His serious thoughts furrowed his handsome face into deep wrinkles.

Chapter 7
SARA THE CAREGIVER

Sara adjusted the bathtub tap to warm and sat down on the edge of the tub, testing the water with her fingers as she absent mindedly watched it filling the gigantic circular, porcelain bathtub in preparation for Tara and Cohen's bath.

My life has become as twisty as a roller coasters ride these the last few weeks. Sara thought nervously. *Here I am in Vancouver, British Columbia caring for two delightful children and getting to spend more time with my son. Soon we'll be on our way to Edmonton, the next leg of the Enlighten journey.*

Sara had been told by Meaghan that the next formal stop was Edmonton, Alberta, but that there would still be some smaller day trips in British Columbia before the big move. *This is a lot of excitement for an old girl like me. But it's fun. I love having Luc around more. I wonder how God will work it all out, with Luc's baby and Lisa and Meaghan. Thankfully I'm not the one in control of all this, its way too much for me!"* Sara thought with a nervous chuckle.

It wasn't the traveling or the children that caused Sara to feel somewhat overwhelmed. Luc had informed Sara about his upcoming date with Lisa.

BLOOMING IN FULL COLOR

I wonder what on earth that woman is up to now! Sara thought. *She's probably realized what a good man she's let get away. Maybe she thinks she's in love with Luc now and wants to get back together and raise their child. Lord, only You know what needs to be done here. I trust that You will provide wisdom for both Luc and Lisa, giving them Your desire in this situation. I place this dilemma in your capable hands, in your precious Son Jesus' name, I pray.*

At that moment Cohen came barrelling into the bathroom, clad solely in his birthday suit. "Can I dive in?" he asked excitedly.

Sara slid her hand down into the water for a temperature test. Nodding her head with eyes fixed warily on Cohen's face, she said. "No diving, just climb in!" She pulled her hand out of the water and sprayed a few drops in Cohen's direction.

Having Sara's permission Cohen climbed up onto the tub edge and jumped into the almost full tub of water with a mighty splash. A giant tsunami rose up out of the bathtub. Sara saw it coming but couldn't move fast enough to get out of its path. She was instantly drenched.

Cohen sat down quickly in the bathtub, and laughed and laughed.

"*Co—hen!* You little rascal! What am I going to do with you?" Sara spluttered, running her wet hands through her saturated hair. Catching a glimpse of herself in the mirror she started laughing too. "What did you do that for?" she asked. "Look at me!"

"I wanted to make a big splash," Cohen said, reaching for a plastic water shooter toy, he began filling the water chamber.

"You made a big splash all right!" Sara replied. "You got me all wet young man, and now it's your turn."

Sara dropped down onto her knees in front of the bathtub, scooped water into her hands and proceeded to drench Cohen. Cohen whirled around in the tub, turning his back toward Sara. He stuck the plug into his loaded water blaster, then flipping himself around with the agility of a three-year-old he aimed it at Sara's chest and pulled the trigger. A stream of water surged forth from the toy making Sara even wetter. She hastily stood up and raised her dripping hands in surrender. "Okay, okay I give up. You win, enough - enough!"

At that moment Tara sauntered nonchalantly into the bathroom. She took a look around and asked indignantly, in her big sister fashion, "What is going on in here? Did you overflow the bathtub, Cohen?"

"I got Sara good n' wet," Cohen exclaimed, giggling gleefully. "I won, 'cause I got her wetter n' she got me."

He then took aim with his water shooter directly at Tara.

"Stop, Cohen. I don't want to play that game." Tara informed him raising her hand as she spoke.

"Okay, I won't squirt you if you play with me. Can we play Noah's ark?" he asked.

"Of course, Cohen, as long as you behave yourself and no more shooting water."

Sara stood up and looked at herself in the bathroom mirror.

"I look worse than a wet rat." She muttered out loud. "Can you two behave yourselves for five minutes while I go and get out of these wet clothes? Maybe I better clean up this mess first."

Grabbing a somewhat dry towel off the rack she tried to sponge the water off her clothes. Not having much luck with that, she once again dropped down on all fours and started sopping up the evidence of the water battle. Letting out a little chuckle she thought, *God, You are so amazing. I was sitting here, all serious and worrying about Luc's problems, and You, the Fixer of all our problems brought this little water warrior into the bathroom totally taking my mind off my problems, that I have no control over anyway! I know You don't want me to worry. Thank You, God, for putting things in perspective. God You are so totally awesome!"*

Chapter 8
LUC – CHOICES

Luc needed some thinking time and decided to head outside for a long walk. Grabbing a light jacket off the hook on his way out the door he was glad he had done so as he soon realized that a warm drizzling rain was beginning to fall. The thoughts in his head were chasing each other around in circles. Luc hoped that God was answering his mother's prayers, in that his baby would be saved from being aborted.

Thank You, God, he thought, *for showing me the truth that if you come right down to it, pregnancy is a consequence, created by our actions and if we are responsible adults we need to find the best possible life solution for the problem.* Luc firmly believed that if the parent couldn't or wouldn't raise a child it should be given a chance to be raised by someone else. Yes, a pregnancy could put a kink in the mother's life for a short time, but isn't that better than terminating the baby's life forever? *It's a human being, for goodness sake, made in the image of God.* Luc knew his passion rose high on this subject.

But now, Luc thought, *Lisa wants to talk. I wonder what that's all about. I really want my relationship with Meaghan to have a chance to grow. But I don't want to make a mistake by rushing things. I want to take it nice and easy.*

Luc came across what looked like a welcoming coffee shop. He wandered in and sat down at a booth. When the waitress came, he said he would like a mug of hot chocolate. Suddenly, becoming aware that he was dripping wet, he lifted up his arms, looking first at one and then the other. Directing his attention out the window he saw that the rain had been coming down harder than he'd realized.

The waitress brought him his requested mug full of steaming hot chocolate, covered with a dollop of whipped cream and chocolate shavings. "You want anything to eat with that hot chocolate, honey?"

"No thanks," Luc replied with a smile. "This is just fine."

"Suit yourself. We got some nice fresh chocolate chip cookies right out of the oven, or maybe some homemade bread, if that tickles your fancy," she continued.

"That sounds delicious, but no thanks. This hot chocolate is all I need for now." Luc answered.

"Well, if you don't mind my sayin'," she continued. "You look like a wet muskrat. There are lotsa paper towels in the bathroom if you want to wipe yourself off."

Luc pulled a couple of serviettes out of the dispenser on the table and rubbed them over his face and hair. "Thanks this will do."

The waitress continued standing with her hand resting on her hip staring at Luc and said once again, "Suit yourself." Finally, she turned and walked away.

Luc took a tentative sip of his chocolate drink, checking on the temperature, perfect! He once again turned his thoughts over to his possible options.

I could be with Lisa and the child, if the child is mine and she hasn't aborted it!

Part of this choice absolutely thrilled him. Being with his child as a full-time father and helping to raise it would be amazing. But maybe the child wasn't his! Was that even a possibility? Or, he could stay where he was and help his mom with Meaghan's two children. He had come to love Cohen and Tara. He knew it would be heartbreaking to leave those two. Never mind leaving Meaghan. He was beginning to have deep feelings for her.

I'm not prepared to give her up, not yet, anyway! He thought. The two of them were becoming good friends, and he loved the sense of companionship they shared. *She brings out the best in me,* he thought. *I could be a part-time dad for Lisa's baby as well though, maybe that would be a good compromise.*

Looking back on his relationship with Lisa, Luc remembered it being totally different than his connection with Meaghan. Lisa worked for the same airline as Luc as a ticket agent in the Saskatoon terminal. He and Lisa had met at a staff party and the physical attraction between them had been instantaneous! They were both single, consenting adults and they'd let their emotions get out of control before they barely knew each other.

With Luc's flight schedule at that time, they managed to be together part of every week. Lisa had always been waiting excitedly for his arrival when he flew into the city. That is until she learned she was pregnant. Then things changed. She became elusive and Luc ran out of ways to try and reach her. *Now what?* He thought.

The waitress wandered over, "You need a refill on that hot chocolate, honey?

It's still raining cats and dogs. You can't go out there in that," she said, pointing to the window.

"No thanks, I'm all done. How much so I owe you?" Luc answered her with a smile. *She really is a good waitress,"* he thought.

"That'll be three dollars, honey."

Luc dug his hand into his pants pocket and pulled out a five dollar bill. Handing it to her he said, "Here you go thanks, keep the change," and made his way toward the door.

"Any time, handsome, you look like you got a lot on your mind."

Luc studied the waitress's face for a moment, and then said, "Yeah, I guess I do." He walked out of the coffee shop and back into the rain.

Oh what a tangled web we weave! He thought.

Chapter 9
MARTY

Marty Summers was stretched out in his favourite recliner, casually flicking through TV channels with the remote. Realizing he'd seen a familiar face flash by he clicked back one channel and there she was. *Is that my Meaghan?* He thought.
What's she doing all dolled up on TV? He started watching the program. "Man, she's lost a ton of weight. Amber, come look at this," he shouted out to his common law companion.

Three years ago, Marty had decided that being married to his high school sweetheart, Meaghan, was not what he had imagined it to be. Marty and Meaghan's visions of marriage were poles apart. Marty couldn't understand the whole concept of "saving up for a rainy day," or "planning for the future." To him it was all about the moment, have fun, play hard. He wasn't gonna have old ideas like his parents. Meaghan just didn't get it! And he didn't get her anymore. She used to be fun, and then she had a kid and decided to get all serious!

A worn-out shadow of a girl with long oily hair strolled into the room. Her petite shoulders were slumped over and she was gently rocking a fevered baby, back and forth, back and forth. Marty glanced up at her, "When's the last time you took a shower and cleaned yourself up?"

"Look!" he exclaimed loudly, pointing at the TV. "That's my ex – she must think she's a movie star or something! Last time I saw her she was big as a whale! Must be nice prancing around on a stage, all dressed up in pretty duds. I wonder who's footin' the bill for her big makeover."

Amber looked at the TV screen, and then back at Marty. She took a deep breath, straightened her shoulders and quietly told him. "For someone as good looking as you are on the outside, inside you're nothing but a big, mean, bully!" Her baby started whimpering and she turned to walk away. As she did so she said over her shoulder. "I'll be in the bedroom. Hopefully this little guy will fall asleep soon, he must be teething. He's burning up and won't stop crying."

Marty let out a grunt and turned the volume higher so he could hear the TV.

The Enlighten Broadcast was over and Marty clicked off the television.

"Now you made me miss the whole program," he announced loudly, "I'm goin' out for a beer."

Amber didn't answer. Marty left the apartment.

Flopping her exhausted body into a hard wooden rocking chair, she cradled her son Billy in her arms. Her body swayed with the rhythm of the chair. Big tears rolled down her cheeks. "What have I done to us, Billy? This is worse than being on our own. He's your daddy and he doesn't even care about us. My mama warned me about men like him, why didn't I listen to her?" She placed a pacifier in Billy's mouth, which he quickly latched on to and began to relax. "Poor little boy, you're worn out. That's my good baby," she crooned. "You have a good sleep; your mama needs a rest too."

Marty left the apartment and walked down the street to the corner bar. The wheels in his head were turning; *maybe it's time to give my sweet Meaghan a call. She's obviously got a good thing goin' on and she's probably hungry for some of ole Marty's lovin'. I sure wouldn't mind givin' up construction work for a while. That jerk of a boss, with all his demands! Makes a guy wanna puke! Expects us to work late and put in overtime, just so he can get the job done quick and* start another one. *The pay's not bad, but who wants to work ten, twelve hours a day? Not me, that's for damn sure!*

Marty's thoughts turned to Amber and Billy. *Amber probably won't care whether I leave or not! She's always got that little brat hanging onta her, he's probably not even my kid!*

Marty smiled as his plan began to take shape in his mind. *I think it's time to get reacquainted with my sweet Meaghan. Life might just get a whole lot easier!*

Chapter 10
LUC AND SARA

Luc and Sara were enjoying their second cup of early morning coffee together.

"Mom, are you sure that taking care of Cohen and Tara is not too much for you? I know they're both usually very busy little people."

"Oh, they're no trouble at all," Sara assured him. "They are such well behaved children and make my life fun. I find myself singing when I'm around them. Meaghan is doing an amazing job raising those two, if you ask me," she added with a chuckle, as she thought of a funny episode with Cohen. "And that makes my job seem like not a job at all, but a Grandma Day."

"Well, that's good to hear, Mom. Tara and Cohen seem like good kids, well behaved and respectful. It's good to know they listen to you when you're alone with them."

"Oh yes, they're no problem at all." Once again Sara assured her son. "Now, tell me about you, what's new with you? Anything happen back in Saskatchewan when you were there?"

"Actually yes, I have some news. But first I want to ask a favour of you. I know it's your day off from child care, and Meaghan did request that she would like to have them all to herself on her days off, but if I were to ask her out on a date tonight and if she were to accept – would you consider babysitting for the evening?"

"Yes, of course I would consider that," Sara chuckled. "You sound nervous – that's not like you. What's going on?"

"I'm really attracted to her, Mom. She's the most unassuming, humble person I've ever met. She doesn't seem to have expectations or make judgements on anyone. I'm sure that people in her life must have let her down and disappointed her, but she carries on with a big smile and a happy attitude. I think she's amazing!"

"Yes, I've noticed that too, Luc. As busy as her life is, and after all she's been through, I never hear her grumbling or complaining, she appears to have a lot of internal peace. Nothing seems to upset that girl."

"Okay, well if you're sure you won't mind babysitting, I'm going to ask her out tonight. I'd like to take Meaghan out to a quiet nightclub so we can sit and talk, seems like we never have time to just sit and enjoy each other's company."

"Now, about my trip to Saskatoon this past week, it was pretty uneventful, just the same old routine when I'm there. I check into my hotel, and then depending on the time of day, I might go for a walk or a jog along the Saskatchewan River. But you know who I'm meeting up with on my next trip to Saskatoon?"

Sara guessed straight away, "Lisa?"

"Yes, Mom, she called and asked if we could meet the next time I'm in Saskatoon."

Sara could hardly contain her excitement and asked, "What is happening with her, Luc? Does she still have the baby? Is everything okay?"

Luc chuckled at his mother's excitement. "I'm not exactly sure, Mom, she wants to talk to me, so I'm thinking she must still be pregnant, or what would we have to talk about? Thank God for that, and thank you Mom, for all your prayers. If she does decide to go ahead and have the baby and wants the two of us to get back together, I'm not sure how I feel about that. I'm giving it some thought though. I know that I don't love her the way I thought I did – but there is a child involved and I think that child deserves a dad. Don't you?"

"Yes, I do Luc, but what about Meaghan and her children? I just heard you say you were falling in love with her, right?"

"I know, Mom. Meaghan and her children are becoming very important to me. I'm not sure what the answer is right now, but I guess I don't even know what the question is! I plan on talking to Meaghan and lay all my cards on the table and see what she has to say about it. That's all I can do, right? She deserves to know the whole truth and I can't leave Lisa and our child high and dry either. I've put myself in a tough spot!"

Chapter 11

FROG SLIPPERS

Luc left his mother's room and walked directly over to Meaghan's room and tapped gently on the door, then waited patiently for a response.

Inside the room Meaghan shuffled to the door. Her feet were covered in big furry green frog slippers, her body clothed in a soft pink terry velour bathrobe and around her head was wrapped a gigantic white bath towel.

Meaghan opened the door a crack and peeked through. "Luc!" She exclaimed in horror, "Nice to see you, but I'm not dressed. When did you get back from Saskatchewan?"

"I got back late last night and I just couldn't wait any longer to see how you and the kids are doing." A big smile spread across Luc's face as he thought about how gorgeous Meaghan looked even without any makeup or hairdo.

"We're all fine. I guess you can come in. Sorry about this!" She said with a self-deprecating gesture. "It's a lazy morning around here. I've just made a pot of coffee. Would you like some?" Meaghan was rubbing the towel nervously through her damp hair.

"Sure, I can handle another cup. I did have coffee with Mom this morning, and that's what brings me over here," Luc said with a mischievous smile. "Mom said she'd be happy to care for Cohen and Tara this evening if you would consider going out with me."

"Go out with you? Like, you mean, on a date?" Meaghan asked, surprised.

She anxiously rewrapped the towel around her hair and with fumbling fingers secured it tightly.

"Well yeah, I guess so. I thought we might go out to a quiet nightclub, maybe order some appetizers and a glass of wine and hang out – do some talking."

Meaghan listened attentively while she poured them each a cup of coffee. She passed one to Luc and looked into his eyes. She was hesitant. Meaghan valued Luc's friendship and wasn't sure she was ready for any changes in their relationship. Yet, it was only a glass of wine and some talking; friends do that all the time.

"Okay, why not? It sounds like fun, if you're sure your mom won't mind watching the kids."

"She says watching the kids' makes her feel young. So who can argue with that – a person can never feel too young, right?" Luc laughed.

Relieved that the question had been asked and Meaghan had accepted, Luc took a big swallow of coffee and then became lost in thought for a moment. Snapping back to the present he fixed his gaze on Meaghan and gave her a warm smile. She looked back at him with a quizzical expression on her face, not quite sure what was going on. They made small talk, while they sipped their coffee.

"Okay then," he said, "Can I come and get you about eight o'clock?"

"I will be ready at eight, Luc, and thanks. I think it will be fun to spend the evening with you,"

Luc was on his way out the door, feeling ecstatic. Meaghan was closing the door behind him when her phone started ringing. Waving her hand in the air, she said, "I better get that. See you at eight." She disappeared into the bedroom to answer the phone.

"Hello!" she said picking up the receiver.

"Hey, Meaghan, this is Cassandra. My husband is away on a business trip this weekend, so I have a free evening. I thought maybe we could go see a movie or something, girl's night out!"

"Oh, Cassandra, you're a few minutes too late. I just make made a date with a very handsome fellow. He wants to take me out tonight."

"Woohoo, lucky you, do I know this handsome man?" Cassandra queried.

"I don't think so. He flies in and out of my life, literally, at the moment. He's the son of my children's caregiver. He's also an airline pilot."

"Well, that sounds very interesting! I'm dying to hear all about him when I see you, but you have fun tonight. Maybe we can do a movie another time."

"That sounds wonderful, Cassandra. Thanks for asking me. I would love to spend more time with you when we have the opportunity. I've always wondered, what did you do before you became the main gal with the Enlighten Weight Loss Program?"

"Actually, I was a court stenographer. I took a two year course right out of high school. The course taught me some introductory law, legal processes and ethics of law. Then because there was a shortage of personnel in this profession, it was easy to get a job," Cassandra replied.

"What an exciting career!"

"Yes, I guess so. But, you know, the courthouse is filled with lots of unhappy or hurting people and many times I found it hard to leave my work at the courthouse."

"Of course, you're right. I never thought of that. It must have been hard. Well when we get together I want to hear all about your transition from courthouse steno to CEO for Enlighten. How did that all come about?"

"It's a long story, Meaghan. But I will tell you all about it sometime. For now I will let you go be with your children." Cassandra told her.

The two women said their goodbyes and signed off.

BLOOMING IN FULL COLOR

Hmmm, a date with Luc tonight! Meaghan thought, and her beautiful hazel eyes began to twinkle.

Chapter 12

SARA REMEMBERING

After Luc left Sara's hotel room she decided to sit right where she was and relax, letting her mind wander over the predicament Luc had gotten himself into.
Lord, I know that all things work together for good to those who love and believe in You. So I will not worry about Luc's situation. You are in control, Heavenly Father and I pray that Your will, shall be done.
Sara felt better after praying and her mind wandered back to her own younger years and some of the issues she had faced in her youth. Sara had been born into what she now realizes was a very poor family in the fifties. Her dad, John Keller drove an old second hand pickup truck to work six days a week at a community sawmill situated in northern Saskatchewan, between the Saskatchewan and Manitoba borders. His skill was to manually plane the knots in birch, poplar and spruce trees that had been made into lumber. He planed the knots until they were smooth and flat.
Sara thought of the old pick-up truck with a smile on her face, remembering that she along with all her brothers and sisters would pile into the back while her dad and mom would sit in the front as they drove to a nearby lake for a refreshing swim. This was their usual Sunday activity in the summer.

Her mother, Grace Keller, stayed at home with her children, which is what most mothers did in those days. There she cared for some neighbour children while their mother went out of the home to work.

She remembers her mother and father either being busy or being tired. Dad would come home from a hard day of work at the sawmill dog tired and Mom, after minding little children eight hours a day was ready to sit down and relax. That left Sara with a lot of free time on her hands.

As a young child, Sara remembers being very adept at keeping herself busy and happy. She loved playing with her dolls or riding her bicycle around the block. Sara had three older sisters and younger twin brothers. Kenny and Freddy, the twins were two years younger than Sara and they loved it when she played with them in their sandbox.

Kenny was the proud owner of a toy road grader and Freddie of a toy gravel truck. The two boys spent endless hours building winding sand roads adorned with stick bridges, and Rocky Mountains landscapes. They hauled many miniature loads of gravel to their construction sites. Sometimes Sara would sit in the sand with the boys and enjoy herself as much as they did. Kenny and Freddie got so excited when she joined them.

It was a happy, peaceful time.

Although Sara was an exemplary student academically, Kenny could top her marks without any effort. He was a very gifted student and Sara remembers feeling disappointed many times after putting in many hours studying for an exam only to receive a lower mark than Kenny in the same subject.

Freddie, on the other hand was not interested in academics whatsoever, but give him any kind of toy with a motor in it and he would have the motor taken out, examined, and put back together before she could say Robinson Crusoe. He had amazing mechanical talent!

But of course as Sara grew closer to becoming a teenager she lost interest in sandboxes and toy road graders and little brothers. She blossomed into a beautiful innocent teenager, totally unaware of the changes that were taking place in her appearance. She was always surprised when adolescent boys appeared interested in her. She considered boys – as well as girls – her friends and hung out with a large group of them whenever she could.

Sara's mind wandered back to the time when her mother Grace became terribly ill. She had lost her appetite and everything she did try to eat (to keep up her strength) wouldn't sit right in her stomach and a few minutes later up it would come. This went on for several months, thus making her mother very thin and weak. Grace didn't have the strength to look after little children anymore and was forced to give up her child care career, spending most of her days and nights in bed.

Then one day, Sara vividly recalls riding along with her mother to the local health care clinic. Sara's older sisters had by this time left home and it was only Sara and her brothers remaining. By the time they reached the clinic, Grace had become so weak from the strain of driving that she didn't have the energy left to go inside. She parked the car, turned off the ignition and her body slumped forward over the steering wheel. Sara panicked, her twelve-year-old legs swung out of the car and she flew inside the clinic to get help.

Once inside, she hysterically told the receptionist, "My mother, needs help, please come!"

The receptionist stood up and hurried into another room with a sign on the door that read "Staff only." Then, as if by magic a man appeared and kindly asked Sara, "Where is your mother?"

Sara remembers her eyes wandering over to the name badge on the man's uniform. It read "Carl."

At the same time Carl was releasing the brakes on a nearby empty wheelchair.

"Mom's in the car, please hurry!" Sara pleaded.

The receptionist, Carl and Sara hurried outside to Grace's car. Carl opened the driver's side door and quickly reached his hand inside and checked the pulse on Sara's mother's neck.

"There's a weak pulse," he said. "Help me get her into the chair."

Carl aligned the wheelchair up beside the car seat, while the receptionist raced around to the passenger side and crawled onto the front seat. Carl awkwardly swung Grace's legs out of the car. The receptionist balanced Grace's head and the two of them managed to lift and wiggle Grace into the chair. Sara stood watching – terrified!

Once back inside the clinic, the receptionist picked up the phone and dialled 911. Carl pushed the wheelchair towards an examining room.

"The doctor will look at your mother!" Carl told Sara. They went inside and closed the door. The receptionist asked Sara where her dad could be reached and then dialled his work number.

Sara waited and waited. An ambulance pulled up and two attendants joined Sara in the waiting area. Sara's dad came – he waited too. Finally, the doctor came out of the room. "I've got her condition stabilized," he announced to everyone present. Nodding towards the ambulance attendants, he continued, "And made arrangements for the ambulance to take her to St. Peter's Hospital."

Sara and her dad rushed over to her mom as the attendants wheeled her past them.

Her eyes were closed and she was very pale.

"I love you, Mom." Sara whispered.

Her dad touched Grace's hand as she was rolled by. "What's wrong with her, doctor?" John asked. "Will she be all right?"

"Well, I can't say for sure," the doctor replied, "But it appears that she has an internal bleed somewhere in her lower intestinal area. Once they get her to the hospital they'll perform some tests to find out what's happening. How long has she been suffering?"

John looked at the doctor and said, "You know I think it's been several months. She never complains, so I don't really know. Can they fix her, doctor? Do you know what caused this? Will she be all right?"

"I'm sure we'll be able to help her, but it may take some time for her to get back to her normal self. I'm not sure what would cause this, maybe an inherited bleeding disorder, sometimes a bump can occur that causes significant bleeding issues – a blood vessel ruptures!" The doctor lifted his hands as he shrugged his shoulders.

John stepped back and held out his hand to the doctor. "Thank you doctor, for what you've done for my wife." They shook hands.

"Come Sara, let's follow that ambulance!" Dad said.

Sara's mind wandered back to the present and she took a sip of her coffee. Thankfully, her mother had made it through the ordeal and life returned to what it was before, almost! During this difficult time, Sara's dad and his family reached out to their church family for comfort and support, and support was given.

Meals were brought to their house, babysitting and house cleaning services were provided by church members, thus easing the load John was forced to carry. Sara remembers praying constantly for her mother, and she was sure that the church family was doing the same.

Looking back, she believes this was the turning point of her faith.

Sara sought out God, in search of consolation. One day she knelt down on the floor beside her bed and told God she was missing something and wanted to be a part of God's family. "I know I'm not perfect God, but I will try to do better, please let me belong to Your family in heaven. I know that You died on the cross for me and You are my personal Saviour." Looking back, Sara realized it was a pretty childish prayer. But God heard her and Sara heard God's choir of angels in heaven rejoicing and singing a beautiful song.

"What's happening?" Sara asked filled with wonder.

And God replied – Sara could hear Him just as plain as day, "YOUR SINS ARE WASHED AWAY, YOU ARE SAVED."

It was the lifeline Sara was looking for.

Chapter 13

MARTY TROUBLE

Meaghan put the phone down from talking to Cassandra and once again it started ringing immediately.

What's going on this morning? Meaghan wondered. *This phone never rings and it appears to be grand central station here today. Cassandra must have forgotten something.*

Reaching for the phone once again she sang a cheery hello, with a smile on her face. A man's deep voice on the other end of the line said, "Hello, Meaghan. How are ya?

I won't keep you guessin', this is your old Marty calling. Thought it was 'bout time you and me got together for a drink and catch up on old times."

"Marty?" Meaghan asked in bewilderment. Meaghan hadn't heard from Marty for over three years. What was going on!

"Yeah, Meaghan, how ya been doin'? I've been thinkin' about ya a lot lately and decided we should prob'ly do some catchin up! What do ya think 'bout that?"

Meaghan was completely dumbfounded. "What could we possibly have to catch up about Marty? You left me for another woman, remember? Actually, from what I hear, there were many women, one after another!"

"Oh that was just a phase I was goin' through. I got it out of my system now and I realize that you're the only one for me!"

Meaghan didn't know what to say. She didn't want to get into a word battle with Marty.

She certainly wasn't interested in meeting with him. That part of her life was over. There was no way she was ever going to try and revive a relationship with a man who had deceived her, lied to her, physically abused her and ridiculed her. There was silence on the phone as Meaghan thought over his request.

Marty started pleading. "Aw c'mon Meaghan, just one drink."

"That won't work out for me, Marty. I have a full schedule of appointments for several weeks; there won't be time to fit in any more."

Marty seemed to be satisfied, "Well, okay for now, sweet Meaghan. I've been readin' about ya in the newspaper and seen ya on TV, you're lookin' mighty fine I must say! We'll leave it until next weekend. Maybe we can work somethin' out then. You know I'll be watchin' ya and thinkin' about ya every minute until then."

Watching me? Thinking about me? That is so creepy! Meaghan thought. "I really don't think there will be time in my schedule for quite a while Marty, they keep me very busy so please don't phone here again!"

She hung up the phone.

Chapter 14
DATE NIGHT

At eight o'clock sharp, Meaghan heard a gentle tapping on her hotel room door.

Outside the door, Luc was nervously pacing while he waited to be let into Meaghan's room and hopefully, her life. Luc feared Meaghan might be somewhat "man shy" after her ordeal with her first husband. He gathered from her comments that she had put up with some pretty nasty treatment from him before their marriage had ended.

On the other side of the door, Meaghan sucked in her breath, gave herself one last primp in the mirror and thought, *Life can certainly get complicated with old relationships and new relationships and families and love and hate and disharmony!* But, she thought, *I remember my dear sister, Hattie, telling me once, 'Take the high road, Meaghan. We must choose to bloom not to be bitter.'*

God, I need You to help me remember to keep things in perspective in my relationship with Luc. Help me to remember You first God and my children next. A friendship with Luc would be an extra blessing. I know it's not Your will that I return to an abusive relationship with Marty.

Meaghan's heart was thumping erratically in her chest as she cautiously opened the door and saw her very handsome date waiting for her. Then she let out a self-conscious laugh as she realized that each of them had decided to wear denim jeans and long sleeved white cotton shirts. They looked at each other and then down at themselves in synchronization.

Luc spoke first with a laugh. "Look at us, we're matching – two great minds think alike!"

Meaghan laughed, "And dress alike!" The only variation in their dress was a soft cashmere scarf in rich mulberry tones draped casually around Meaghan's neck.

Luc was wearing his shirt open at the neck with the top three buttons left undone.

Stepping inside the room, Luc quickly caught Cohen in his arms as the youngster came barrelling out of the bathroom. Tara followed quietly behind him.

"Hello there, buckaroo," Luc said ruffling Cohen's hair.

"I'm not buckaroo, I'm Cohen," he stated.

Luc laughed, "Of course you are and hello there beautiful princess, how are you?" He asked, turning his attention to Tara.

Color slowly crept into Tara's cheeks as she replied, "Hello Luc, did you come over to play games with us tonight?"

"Not tonight, honey. I came to take your mother out. Sara is coming over to play some games with you."

"I'm right here, Luc," Sara said stepping into the room. "I was just mopping up the bathroom after these two fish had their swim. I think there was more water on the floor than in the tub. Cohen never gets tired of the splashing game, but that's okay, it's only water, and the bathroom gets a thorough cleaning every day."

"You're a good sport, Mom. Were you always this patient with us when I was kid?" Luc asked.

"I like to think I always had lots of patience with you and your siblings. The older I get the more I realize how precious children are, so it's easy to nurture these two. When you were a kid, some days it seemed like you would never grow up. And look at you now. Here you are all grown up and actually appreciating your mother. Who would have thunk it?"

Luc smiled at his mother and then turned his attention to Meaghan. "Well, are we ready to go?"

"Yes, I think we are. What about you Sara, any questions before we leave?" Meaghan asked.

"I think we're all good, right you two? Anything we need to know before your mom leaves?"

Cohen piped up, "Luc will you come over and play games with us tomorrow?"

"Sure, I would love to do that Cohen. Tomorrow we will have a play date, maybe we can go over to the park and play some games," Luc answered.

"You're not lying or tricking me, are you?" Cohen asked.

Luc chuckled and answered. "Of course not, buddy. I'll be happy to take you and Tara out on a date tomorrow. It will be just the three of us, no moms or grammas allowed."

Tara and Cohen's eyes lit up and both of them started jumping up and down, squealing with excitement.

"I think they like that idea a lot," Meaghan said.

"Now I want you to be good listeners to Sara. When she says its bedtime, then you have to listen. You'll be asleep when I get home, so goodnight. I'll see you in the morning." Meaghan bent over and kissed and hugged each of her children.

Luc held out his hand and they jumped up to give him a high five. "I'll see you two tomorrow," he said.

He kissed his mother on the cheek; Meaghan grabbed her room key off the shelf by the door, shoved it into her little shoulder bag and the two of them left.

Chapter 15

MARIO'S BAR AND GRILL

Once outside the hotel, Luc grabbed Meaghan's hand and then with his free hand hailed a cab. Immediately, a taxi pulled up to the curb beside them and Luc held the door open for Meaghan, they quickly climbed inside.

"Where to, boss?" the cabby asked.

"Mario's Bar and Grill" Luc responded.

"Nice place!" the cabby added and then carefully pulled out into the busy evening traffic.

As they travelled to Mario's, Luc began telling Meaghan how he'd come across the bar one day while he was out walking along the Fraser River. "I stopped in to order a hot chocolate. It was another damp, foggy day and I felt chilled, so I ducked into Mario's to get warmed up and couldn't believe how pleasant and welcoming it felt in there. It was in the middle of the afternoon and they were taking freshly-baked cookies and bread out of the ovens. They offered me a cookie along with my hot chocolate, smart move on their part and the aromas reminded me of growing up when my mom used to bake bread."

Meaghan looked up at Luc and responded with a smile, "How nice! Maybe we can have some tonight, you're making me hungry for fresh bread."

The cabby announced, "Here we are, that'll be twelve dollars please."

Luc pulled fifteen dollars out of his wallet and passed it to the driver. "Here you go, thanks for the ride and have a good evening!"

The couple stepped out of the cab; the cabby saluted, said thanks and drove off into the night.

Meaghan and Luc entered Mario's, where the Club's hostess quickly approached and asked them if they wished to be seated by the fireplace or by the windows overlooking the Fraser River.

"You decide," Luc said to Meaghan. "I'm fine with either one."

"Let's sit by the fire, if that's okay. I love the glow and warmth of a fire."

Once seated, Luc and Meaghan each ordered a glass of Malbec and Luc requested some freshly-baked bread and cheese to go along with the wine.

The hostess replied, "Our baker baked some specialty breads today. Is there any particular kind you would you like?" She went over the list of their baked goods; it was a tough decision but Meaghan ended up choosing light rye and Luc chose the homemade white bread with lots of butter.

Once the hostess left Meaghan let out a long sigh, settled back in her soft leather chair, and began to relax. "You know I was just thinking, that the last time I was out with a man – which was my husband – we went to a restaurant for dinner and never made it through the first course. He told me he wanted out of our marriage. I hope I don't have the same effect on you and you dump me before the drinks come!"

"I would never do that, Meaghan! I'm sorry that it happened," Luc replied.

Meaghan continued, "You know, it shouldn't have been a big surprise. Our marriage wasn't good for a long time before that, but I wanted to believe that we could work out our differences. Anyway, that was a long time ago and I've tried to stop feeling guilty. It was his choice, not mine."

"I don't know what to say, Meaghan. You do have two beautiful children. I'd say you definitely came out the winner."

"Yes I know, my children are the best. It hasn't been easy, being a single parent but they're worth every second of my time and energy and love."

"Does their father ever make any attempt to see Tara and Cohen?"

"He hasn't, not since the day he left." Meaghan paused and looked directly at Luc. "That is, until, today! He called and told me he was interested in us getting back together."

Luc looked into Meaghan's eyes. "And how do you feel about that?"

Just then the waiter approached with their wine and fresh bread.

"Ooh, that smells wonderful!" Meaghan gushed.

The waiter proceeded to place the goods dramatically on their table. Along with the bread, he produced a beautiful, small ceramic bowl full of whipped butter and a matching ceramic plate containing various cheese samples. He poured a sample of wine in each glass for them to taste and then stood back to await their response. Luc and Meaghan both approved of their choice and nodded to the waiter, who filled their glasses. Then with a bow, he backed away and told them he would be back soon.

Meaghan quickly reached for a slice of the fresh rye bread, broke off a chunk, swished it in the butter and stuffed it into her mouth. "Uumm yummy," she said with her mouth full.

"You're starving!" Luc laughed and said, pulling off a piece of soft white bread and doing exactly the same thing.

"No, I wouldn't say starving!" Meaghan replied with a smile. "I'm just hungry for something familiar and homemade after eating hotel meals for the past four weeks. You know I used to do lots of baking and cooking."

"No, I didn't know that Meaghan, but I do know what you mean by having cravings for this homemade food, it's a real treat!" Luc responded.

Luc and Meaghan sat back and enjoyed their bread with butter and cheese. The fireplace gave off a warm, relaxing atmosphere and the couple felt peaceful and content.

"This is a great way to spend a Friday evening!" Meaghan exclaimed, as she reached for another piece of bread and began buttering. But guess I better go easy on this, if I want to keep my job!"

"I'm glad it worked out for both of us. You know with my schedule, I don't always get weekends off and then it's just not possible for me to be out drinking wine if I have to be flying the next day!"

"Of course, I never even thought of that. And I suppose if a person did this all the time it might lose its charm, but it's just what I needed tonight. Oh look, they're setting up the stage for the entertainment."

A lone troubadour ambled onto the stage and perched himself onto a wooden stool while a stagehand stepped up and connected the speakers and turned on a spotlight. The entertainer slowly strummed his guitar, and then launched into his version of "Love Me Tender, Love Me True" by Elvis Presley.

Meaghan and Luc listened to his first number with enjoyment.

Then Meaghan looked into Luc's eyes and said, "I'm not trying to avoid your question about Marty being in my life again. Actually, I've been giving it a lot of thought. I'm not against him being a part of the children's lives; however there has to be some guidelines. He hasn't shown any responsibility towards the children so far and I will not get back together with him as his partner," she added.

"If he wants visitation with the children there has to be a supervisor present at least until he proves himself. And I would definitely want to know where they are at all times. I won't have him popping into their lives haphazardly whenever he gets the urge. There has to be some consistency. I think that's only fair to Tara and Cohen!"

"Have you told him this?" Luc asked.

"Not yet, he only called this morning, pleading that we should get together to discuss old times." Meaghan shrugged her shoulders. "Marty can be very unpredictable." I'm not sure if he ever will call back."

"Well, it sounds like you've put some serious thought and sound judgement into your decision! And now young lady would you like to dance? This song is calling us onto the dance floor."

Meaghan brushed the bread crumbs from her hands onto her napkin and with a happy smile on her face rose up and melted into Luc's arms for a slow easy waltz. Luc and Meaghan swayed slowly from side to side in time to the music.

"Ah Luc, this is so wonderful and peaceful!" Meaghan breathed softly next to Luc's ear. "I've forgotten what it's like to have a night out with another adult and do grown-up stuff, like dancing." She pulled back from Luc and looked into his eyes; her own eyes were dancing with happiness.

Luc studied Meaghan's face and said, "You're right Meaghan, it's fantastic, and you look amazing, by the way!" Luc felt himself melting as he looked into Meaghan's beautiful green eyes.

Meaghan smiled up at Luc. "Thank you so much, kind sir. You look very smashing yourself!"

The music ended on a sweet note and the duo made their way back to their seats.

"Are you ready for another glass of wine?" Luc asked his partner.

"No thanks, I'm okay for now." Meaghan replied. She felt like she was doing a lot of smiling this evening, which was unusual for her. Basically she was a happy person, but her life for the past three or four years had been all about her children and her job and while that was all very enjoyable often she felt that life was way too serious and much too busy. "Wouldn't it be nice to have more time for fun?" she said to no one in particular.

"Pardon me?" Luc asked her. "What did you say?"

Meaghan wasn't sure she wanted to get into such a deep conversation at this moment, but it was weighing on her mind so she decided to pursue the topic.

"I just wondered out loud, why do we take life so seriously? Shouldn't we be having more fun along the way?" Meaghan replied with a wistful smile.

They arrived at their table and Luc pulled out Meaghan's chair for her. Once they were both seated, he looked steadily into her eyes for a few seconds. "I'm surprised you asked that question," he said. "I thought that with your two adorable children you were probably enjoying a laugh a minute!"

Meaghan chuckled and said, "Of course Tara and Cohen bring me lots of joy. I love everything they say and do, but it's a great responsibility being a single parent. Their dad doesn't pay any child support, so there's always been the financial issue of having enough money to pay the bills. Then of course the energy required being both a mother and father. I've never looked at my situation as just getting by. I've always felt that Tara and Cohen deserve more. I want their childhood to be fun and exciting and stimulating! I want to make memories with them that they will never forget. I'm trying to teach my children about God and life and making good choices; the kind of choices that will carry them through their tough teenage years and then on to make wise decisions as adults. So far, we've met and conquered many challenges. Thankfully, God has been very good to us, providing this job with the Enlighten Weight Loss Program is certainly a wonderful blessing and for the first time in a few years I don't have to worry about finances, and that's a very huge relief."

Luc studied Meaghan and was awed by what she had just said. *What a wonderful, courageous, person she is,* he thought. He was so impressed with Meaghan's little speech that he remained silent for a couple of minutes. Then acknowledging her comments he said, "I am amazed, Meaghan, by your desires and compassion for your children. I've never been a parent of course, so I have no knowledge of that role, but I feel that if I were I would certainly feel the same way as you – wanting my children to be happy and teaching them to be the best they can be as well as learning the life skills required to be true to yourself as an adult.

"Which brings me to the subject I need to talk to you about, Meaghan. There's something I need to share with you!" Luc gently informed his companion.

Chapter 16
BABY NEWS

"Intriguing!" Meaghan exclaimed, with a mischievous grin on her face. "Please tell!"

Luc reached over and took hold of Meaghan's tiny hand that had been resting on the crisp white tablecloth. Picking it up gently, he studied it carefully for a moment and then began recounting his tale about the situation with Lisa.

He paused, looking up for Meaghan's reaction.

Meaghan's expression remained stoic. She waited to hear more.

"At first, she was all about having the baby aborted; she didn't want to bother with it. But now, thankfully, I don't think she's going in that direction any longer." Luc started to say something else and then abruptly closed his mouth; falling silent, not knowing what else to say.

"What are your plans?" Meaghan asked. Her voice filled kindness and compassion.

"At this particular moment, I have no plans. If this baby is mine, I would like to be a part of his life. My feelings about Lisa have changed since I met you. I can't go back to a relationship with her," Luc solemnly informed Meaghan.

"Oh Luc, you know that as much as we like each other as friends we are a long way from making any long-term commitments!" Meaghan exclaimed.

"Yes, I know that, Meaghan," Luc said with a half smile. "But our relationship feels right to me. It seems like you are the piece of the puzzle – so to speak – that's been missing from my life. I feel whole when I'm with you, and you know that I love your children. They are so adorable and well behaved. You're doing a great job with them."

Meaghan laughed. "Thanks Luc, you're right about my kids, they are very special. They keep me grounded."

"I admire you for that. So that brings us back to my situation. What about my child and its needs? Where will I place it on my list of priorities, especially since I won't be living with his mother?"

Meaghan held up her hands and shrugged her shoulders. "That I don't know, Luc. It's something you and Lisa will have to come to terms with."

"That's what I like about you, Meaghan. You're so positive, no condemnation, no rebuke, you just deal with the facts in the best way possible. That's a great quality coming from a very wise person," Luc stated, staring into Meaghan's hazel eyes once again.

Meaghan let out a little laugh. "Well, I don't think I would go that far. I'm a long way from being wise, but there are only a handful of ways to deal with any situation, so why not take the high road and try to make the best out of one's circumstances?"

"Sounds like very good advice to me, Meaghan. I'll try to remember that tidbit of advice. Now will you do me the honour of having another dance with me?"

"I would love to dance with you, sir." Meaghan demurely replied, batting her eyelashes at Luc.

The couple danced and talked and danced some more until the clock could be heard striking midnight.

"This has been a wonderful evening, Luc. Thanks. Now I think it's time to be getting back to reality. I would love to do this again sometime though. It's been so much fun, a great way to unwind and relax and thanks to your mom, I never spent one moment worrying about the children."

"Okay, Meaghan. I will take you home but we will definitely do this again, I've enjoyed it more than I can say." They stood up together and Luc wrapped his arm possessively around Meaghan's shoulders and squeezed them firmly. Paying their bar tab on the way out, they walked into the starry night and hailed a taxi for the ride back to their hotel.

Chapter 17
POPEYE'S PANCAKES

Saturday morning arrived clear and tranquil.

Luc looked out of his hotel window at seven o'clock to check on the weather and decided it would be a wonderful day to take Tara and Cohen on an outdoor adventure. *Just the three of us,* he thought. *No time for my usual leisurely cup of coffee and newspaper this morning. I'm sure those two will be up and ready to go.*

Luc hurried into the shower, then gave himself a quick shave and got dressed.

He was excited to have part of the day with Tara and Cohen. He knew he dare not keep them for the whole day but four or five hours would give them plenty of time to have an exciting escapade. Luc caught himself smiling as he looked into the mirror and thanked God for bringing Meaghan's family into his life!

We'll start with pancakes, he thought. *Kids love pancakes!*

Hurrying out the door, he walked over to Meaghan's room and knocked lightly.

Meaghan answered the knock with Tara and Cohen peering out from behind her.

"Good morning everyone," Luc greeted them cheerfully.

"Good morning, Luc!" both children and their mother responded in unison.

Meaghan was smiling up at Luc. He returned her smile.

"Can we go now?" Cohen asked. "We're all ready to go; we've been waiting all morning for you!"

"Of course we can, that's why I'm here. Tara are you ready?" Luc replied.

"Yes, I'm ready. Can we go to Popeye's Pancake Place for breakfast, Luc?"

"Popeye's Pancakes, sure we can if that's what you want," Luc assured her.

"Yay, pancakes!" Cohen shouted.

"Easy young man, no one here is deaf, please use your indoor voice," Meaghan warned.

"Sorry, Mom," Cohen replied, "I'm so 'cited, I forgot!"

"That's okay, you three better go find some pancakes, I think I'm going back to bed for another hour!" Meaghan informed them.

"Bye, Mom. See you later. Have a good sleep." Cohen told her.

"Do you want us to bring you some pancakes, Mom?" Tara asked.

"Oh no, honey, I'm okay. I'll find something to eat here when I get hungry. You just go eat and have lots of fun. I'll be here when you get back." Meaghan assured them.

Luc, Tara and Cohen caught the elevator to the ground floor and headed in the direction of Popeye's.

"So do you two have any ideas of what you'd like to do after breakfast?" Luc asked.

"Can we go to a movie? Mom never has time to take us to a movie," Tara asked.

"What about you Cohen, do you have any requests?" Luc inquired.

"Nah, I don't care what we do. I just wanna be with you, Luc. Can we spend the whole day together?" Cohen replied grabbing on to Luc's big hand and holding tightly.

Aw, what a sweet little boy, Luc thought and then asked Tara, "What movie would you like to see?"

"Can we see Frozen? I haven't seen that movie yet and it's got princesses in it. I *love* movies with princesses," Tara replied.

"It's okay with me Tara, how about you Cohen, are you okay with the movie Frozen?" Luc asked him.

"Is anybody else in the movie 'side princesses?" Cohen asked.

"I saw the preview on TV, and there's a snowman and a big elk or moose or something like that," Tara replied gesturing extensively with her arms.

"Okay, we can see Frozen; I never saw a elk or a moose in a movie afore, but I'm hungry," Cohen stated.

Luc chuckled at Cohen's grammar and hung on to their hands tightly as the threesome hurried along, a child skipping on either side of him.

"There's Popeye's," Tara announced, spying the overhead sign.

Once inside the restaurant they were quickly seated and Popeye himself came over to their table to take their order. Cohen was speechless. Popeye was a new character in his world and he wasn't sure how to respond.

"Can I take yer order?" Popeye demanded and with an oversized wink at Luc he continued, "I'm sure you'll be wantin' spinach fer yer breakfast?"

Tara glanced at Luc with wide eyes and shook her head, saying "Luc, not spinach please, I really want blueberry pancakes with sweet syrup."

"I don't want spinach!" Cohen stated. "I want pancakes."

Popeye flexed his biceps and asked the children, "Don't you wanna have big muscles like Popeye? Spinach gives you huge muscles!"

"No thanks, we want pancakes, please!" Tara quietly but firmly replied.

"Okay, pancakes for the youngsters, what about you, sir? Can I interest you in spinach?" Popeye asked Luc.

"No spinach for me either, we'll all have pancakes, Popeye, and orange juice and a coffee for me, please." Luc said.

"Pancakes it is then. I'll be back with them before you know it!" Popeye said and hurried away.

"I thought he really was going to make us eat spinach," Tara said.

"I think he was just teasing us," Luc assured her.

Soon, Olive, Popeye's sweetheart arrived carrying a little baby. She was walking along beside Popeye, who was carrying a loaded tray with everyone's order. She smiled at the children and proudly introduced her baby, "This is my baby, Sweet Pea," she said. The baby was dressed in bright red pyjamas that flowed down over its feet. On her bald head the baby wore a tiny white sailor hat with a black velvet band around the brim, identical to Popeye's. Cohen had never seen a baby look like this before and he let out a little laugh.

Luc quickly put his hand over Cohen's on the table and gave it a tight squeeze. Looking up at Luc, Cohen stopped laughing and Luc hastily said, "What a delightful little baby you have. How old is she?"

Olive announced with a proud look on her face, "Today is Sweet Pea's Birthday; she is one year old!"

"Then we must sing to Sweet Pea," Luc said. "Tara and Cohen, let's sing happy birthday to Sweet Pea." And so they did.

Sweet Pea seemed to like the attention. She clapped her little hands and rewarded them with a toothless grin.

Olive was very tall and perfectly slender. Her jet black hair was parted in the middle, pulled back from her face and formed into a miniature bun, which looked like a little olive sitting on the top of her head. Her long totally straight eggplant purple skirt ended at her ankles and on her feet she wore thick clunky brilliant green patent platform shoes. Tara looked her up and she looked her down. She had never seen anyone dressed like Olive before and she wasn't sure what to think. She did admire Olive's blouse. It was pure white with a delicate little round lace collar and tiny pearl buttons decorating the front.

Olive passed the baby to Popeye and exclaimed, "Now blueberry pancakes for the princess, and regular pancakes for the two strong handsome men, orange juice for everyone, and one coffee. Can we get you anything else?"

The children were famished and dug into their meals without uttering a word. Luc thanked Olive and Popeye who then scurried away with little Sweet Pea. Luc enjoyed watching Tara and Cohen get pleasure from their meals and he felt at peace.

"What should we do next?" Luc asked. "The movie won't be playing until this afternoon so we have some time for another activity before the movie. Cohen have you thought of anything you'd like to do?"

"I know, Luc. Could we go to that big building where they keep all the books and find some books to take home to read? We even get to sit and read books there, if we want to. Gabrielle takes us there and sometimes she lets us play games on the 'puter. Can we go there, Luc?" Cohen asked excitedly.

Is Gabrielle your teacher?' Luc asked.

Cohen piped up, "Yes, she's our teacher and she's learning us about Loons. They are big, black birds that swim on a lake and have a white circle round their necks."

"That's interesting, Cohen. Tara did you learn anything about the Loon?"

"Yes, they live in northern Saskatchewan in the summer, but I'm not exactly sure where they go in the winter. Do you remember where they go, Cohen?" Tara asked.

Cohen had lost interest in the Loon talk and didn't answer her question. "Can we go now, can we go to the book building, please Luc?" he asked.

"Sure we can, buddy. We just need to wait for Popeye to bring us a bill and then after I pay him for breakfast we can leave," Luc assured him.

"Yay!" Cohen shouted.

Tara politely thanked Luc for breakfast and when Cohen heard Tara thanking Luc, he said, "Thanks for pancakes, Luc. They're really good. I like having breakfast with you."

Luc mussed Cohen's hair with his big hand and overcome with emotion, he said, "You're both very welcome. I like having breakfast with both of you. We'll do it again sometime."

Popeye popped over with their bill. Luc paid it and they left the establishment.

"The blueberry pancakes were great!" Tara said.

"Yes it was very enjoyable. You two were very well behaved and polite, I'm proud of you," Luc told them.

Luc lifted his arm and hailed a taxi. A bright yellow cab pulled up almost immediately and stopped beside them. "Can you take us to the nearest public library?" Luc asked the driver.

"Of course sir, it's not far," the driver responded.

"We never get to ride a taxi." Cohen gravely told Luc. "We always have to ride a city bus."

"Riding on the bus is fun, Cohen, you like it," Tara informed them.

"Do you like riding on the bus, Cohen?" Luc asked him.

"Yeah, it's okay, I like watching all the people. Sometimes kids ride on the bus without a adult. Do you think kids should ride on the bus without a adult, Luc?"

"Well, not if they're too young, but once they're ten or eleven years old they're probably old enough. How old are these kids, Cohen?"

"I don't know. When I'm ten can I ride on the bus by myself, Luc? Cohen asked.

"That will be your mother's decision. I see the library. We're almost there. I haven't been in a library for a long time. You'll have to show me what to do," Luc informed his young friends. As the taxi came to a stop he paid the driver and they hopped out.

"Let's go," he said grabbing Tara and Cohen's hands, "Come on!"

The trio spent the morning enjoying the library's many activities. First of all Tara and Cohen plunked themselves down in front of a computer where they played word games and number games appropriate for their ages. Luc watched. When they became bored with that activity the three of them headed over to the children's book section.

In the middle of this area sat a large reproduction of a wooden sailing vessel. Each child scurried off to look for some books that interested them. Upon finding them they returned to the ship where Luc was waiting. Amid oversized floor cushions they cuddled up with Luc on the ship's deck and he softly read them stories. Luc noticed Cohen's eye lids getting heavy and gently eased him down onto his own cushion. It wasn't long before Cohen was fast asleep.

Tara decided to go searching for some books to take home with her. Luc told her that was fine but not to go too far away. "I want to see where you are all the time!" he told her.

"I know Luc, that's what Gabrielle always tells us. How long before we go to the movie?" Tara asked.

"I'll just check out the movie times on my phone while you look for some books, okay?" Luc replied.

"Okay, I'll be right over there," Tara said pointing towards a wall of books.

Luc found "Frozen" was showing at 12:30 p.m. at a theatre near the library. They would be able to walk to the movie. *That's lucky,* he thought. Glancing at the time on his phone, he realized that it was 11:30 a.m. so they had one hour.

I'll text Meaghan and let her know what we're up to. I can take the kids home after the movie, so we should be home by three o'clock for sure, he thought.

He texted Meaghan and informed her of their plans.

Tara came back with her arms full of books just as Cohen opened his sleepy eyes.

He spied Luc watching him and scuttled over and climbed onto Luc's lap. Tara sidled up to Luc and sat down on a corner of his cushion as close as she could.

"Can we read this one?" Tara asked pointing to a book with a Loon on it.

"Sure we can, that's a great idea," Luc replied. "We have about half an hour and then we'll walk over to the movie theatre. Is anybody getting hungry or should we just wait and get some popcorn at the theatre?"

"Popcorn," they both shouted.

"Okay, I know popcorn isn't terribly nutritious, but I guess for one day it will be okay. I texted your mom and told her we were going to the movie, but I haven't heard back from her yet," Luc informed the children.

"Can we ask her to come to the movie with us?" Tara queried.

Luc was surprised with this request. He assumed he would be alone with the children for the day. But he liked the idea of Meaghan coming to the movie.

"Is that all right with you Cohen, if your mom comes to the movie with us?" Luc asked.

"Yeah, its okay, but you stay too," Cohen answered, snuggling into Luc's warm chest cavity.

"Okay, I'll text her and ask her if she wants to come with us, then we'll read about this Loon bird," Luc said.

Luc sent a text to Meaghan asking her if she'd like to meet them at the movie theatre and then the three of them snuggled together and read the book.

"The Common Loon is a powerful agile diver diving down into the swift underwater currents to catch small fish to eat. They are less suited to land and go ashore only to nest. They travel north in early spring and breed in April or May where they live for about six months of the year.

"In October or November, the Loon will fly south to get to a warmer climate. One documented case has a Loon flying six hundred and seventy miles in twenty-four hours.

Another case has a Loon travelling three hundred and sixty miles and five hundred and five miles during two consecutive days. All of these flights are single movements.

"Wow isn't that amazing?" Luc asked the children. "That is a lot of miles in one day."

"Where do they spend the winter?" Tara asked.

"Let's see," Luc replied. "It says here they spend the winter along the Atlantic or Pacific coasts or the Gulf of Mexico. Some stay at large reservoirs of water or slow moving rivers."

Luc closed the book and said, "Okay, boy and girl it's time to start walking to the movie theatre. Let's all take a bathroom break before we leave and then we'll check out your books."

Bathroom break and book checkout accomplished they headed out the door.

Meaghan had agreed to meet them at the movie theatre and everyone was excited.

Luc purchased two adult and two children's theatre tickets and then waited in the concession line for popcorn and drinks.

Tara started waving as she spied her mother entering the theatre lobby. Meaghan spotted them and hurried over with a big smile on her face.

"I'm so happy you invited me to come," she said hugging her children. "I thought you wanted to have a day off from your old mother."

Luc turned to Meaghan and gave her a warm smile, "We're all glad you decided to come with us," he said.

Loaded down with the treats the foursome headed into the theatre marked "Frozen." Tara was so excited, she was skipping beside them.

Meaghan walked midway down the rows of seats and chose a row to sit in.

Halfway into the row, she sat down and asked, "Will this be okay?"

Tara sat down next to Meaghan. Luc left an empty seat next to Tara and sat down in the seat after that one. Cohen climbed onto Luc's lap. Luc was juggling bags of popcorn and drinks and library books so he asked Cohen if he could hop off for a minute.

"Why don't you sit in this chair while we eat our popcorn, Cohen? When the movie starts you can sit on my lap, okay?"

Cohen cooperated and climbed into the empty seat. Luc passed out the popcorn and drinks. Everyone got busy eating.

BLOOMING IN FULL COLOR

Tara immensely enjoyed the movie. She loved the princesses, Elsa and Anna. Cohen, snuggled up in Luc's lap, liked the parts with the snowman named Olaf. He thought it was very funny when Olaf kept losing his head.

Luc and Meaghan enjoyed watching the children enjoy the movie. It was a fun film. After the movie, the children asked if Luc and their mom would take them to the swimming pool at their hotel. The adults agreed that was a great idea and off they went.

Luc was amazed at the good time he was having with Tara and Cohen and now their mother. Everyone got along really well. Whenever there were disagreements they seemed to work it out peacefully. Luc liked that.

They arrived by taxi at their hotel and agreed to meet at the pool in a few minutes after getting their swimsuits.

Luc helped Tara carry the heavy bag of library books to their room and then he left them. Finding his swimsuit he decided to put it on with a pair of shorts and t-shirt over top. *Those kids are great!* He thought.

Soon they were all gathered around the pool. Tara and Cohen said at the same time, "Thanks Luc, for taking us on a fun adventure day."

"I liked the blueberry pancakes and the movie the best," Tara told Luc and then added, "And the library was fun too."

Then Cohen piped up, "I liked the pancakes and Popeye and the library and the snowman and the moose and sitting on your lap, Luc. You're the best."

Luc looked at Meaghan and felt his heart overflowing with love. He knew he had fallen deeply in love, not once, not twice but three times. Meaghan and Tara and Cohen had each captured a piece of his heart.

Chapter 18
MEAGHAN

Monday morning Meaghan woke early and stretched her arms long and leisurely towards the ceiling. Her mind wandered back to Friday night and her date with Luc. Luc's dilemma with his ex-girlfriend came to her mind, but she shook her ahead, realizing she did not want to take on that sticky situation.

Meaghan said a silent prayer asking God to guide Luc and Lisa to make the best decisions concerning the unborn baby and their relationship. She decided to leave the situation to God and felt much more peaceful.

Relaxing, she closed her eyes, and let out an extensive yawn. The next thing she knew both her children came flying into her bed, ready to play. Meaghan laughed and started tickling them. She really didn't have time for horse play this morning, but the temptation was great and she decided to give in to it for a few moments. Meaghan remembered it was on her schedule to hit the gym this morning and she dared not be late for Tony, her personal trainer. Tony would be waiting for her exactly at 8:00 a.m. Meaghan had never been late for a date with Tony, but she could sense his wrath if any of his time was wasted.

"Hey you two, enough already, I have to get to work," Meaghan laughed, giving each of them a big juicy kiss on their round rosy cheeks.

"Can we come with you?" Tara asked, looking seriously into Meaghan's eyes.

"You want to come with me?" Meaghan questioned with eyebrows raised. This was something new!

"Yeah, can we come, please?" Cohen chimed in.

Meaghan was taken by surprise. She thought for a moment and then said. "What about your school work and Sara?"

"Sara can come too," Cohen replied.

"Let me think about it while I get ready. You two get into the kitchen and see if Sara has fixed some breakfast for you. Now scram!" Meaghan swatted them on their little bottoms and they ran out of her bedroom.

Jumping out of bed, Meaghan quickly slid into her workout clothes. Breakfast usually consisted of a cup of chopped fresh fruit along with a small yogurt.

"Morning, Sara," Meaghan said as she wandered into the kitchen and started preparing her meal. "Did the kids tell you what's on their mind today?"

"Good morning, Meaghan! And isn't it a beautiful one. Look at that sunshine out there!" Sara responded.

"Yes, indeed it is going to be a beautiful one. Thank you, Lord." Meaghan replied.

"Mom, you're always thanking God for something!" Tara stated.

"Yes, I am and don't you forget to thank God too. He loves it when we appreciate all He does for us." Meaghan replied with a smile aimed at Tara.

Preparations complete, the foursome sat down to enjoy their meal together. After swallowing her first bite, Sara asked, "What do my two beautiful charges have on their minds today?" not being able to stand the suspense any longer.

Tara replied solemnly, "We want to go to the gym with Mom today. It would be fun to work out and play some games. Can we go, can we go? *Puleeese?*"

"I think that's a great idea, don't you Meaghan?" Sara replied. "I have a few errands I can do this morning. Your teacher, Gabrielle can take you to the gym. I'm sure she will have a great workout routine for you. Do you think the formidable Tony will mind, Meaghan?"

Meaghan had hired a tutor for the children, a young Mexican girl with beautiful dark hair and olive skin. Tara and Cohen loved her and Meaghan appreciated the wonderful job the girl was doing with their schooling.

"Well I can't say for sure, but as long as you two stay with Gabrielle and don't interrupt my training session I can't see why it should be a problem!" Meaghan answered.

"Yay!" Tara and Cohen both replied at once and Cohen started racing around the kitchen, he was so excited.

Meaghan reached out and held him still. "Hey, young man, not in here, you wait until you get to the gym, okay?"

"Okay Mom, I will." Cohen replied. "We won't bodder you, Mom!"

"I know you won't, buddy, you will be so busy working out yourself. This is going to be a great day. Give me a high five." Meaghan slapped Cohen's outstretched hand and then reached over to slap Tara's as well.

Breakfast complete Sara shooed the children into their rooms to get ready for the day. "Don't forget to brush your teeth!" She admonished them. Quickly tidying up the kitchen she then left for her own room, humming softly as she went.

Chapter 19
HUNTING FOR TREASURE

Luc's going to Saskatoon today and he'll be there for four days, Meaghan thought. *I hope he and Lisa can get their issues straightened out. Although I can't imagine how that's going to work out, unless they get back together!* Meaghan thought about that scenario and it disturbed her. *I think I'm quite beginning to fall for this tall, dark handsome man. He's pretty easy to be around. I like the way he treats me and the kids, and I like the way he treats his mother. You can always tell how nice a guy is by the way he respects his mother.* Meaghan and Sara both knew his agenda, and were equally concerned about "what could happen!"

Meaghan was pleased that Tara and Cohen were settling into a comfortable routine with Sara and Gabrielle and felt confident they were providing the best possible care for them. Meaghan let out a silent prayer to God, thanking him for the abundance of blessings her family was receiving.

Tara was a quick learner, grasping on to learning concepts easily. She was taking classes in reading, spelling and arithmetic as well as printing, science and health. The classes alternated every second day. Cohen, being only three was being taught his numbers and letters and the sounds of those letters. He was learning how to stay in the lines for coloring and on the lines for printing. He was a willing student and looked forward to Gabrielle's positive praise when he accomplished his desired task. Every third or fourth day, Gabrielle would throw in an art class. Sometimes they would take the bus to an art museum and view art displays and at least twice a week they would get to go to the hotel's swimming pool for exercise and a physical education class. Sometimes they crossed the street to the park where Gabrielle attempted to teach them some soccer skills.

The children loved these extra activities.

Friday's often held a special treat for the children. The young teacher frequently took the twosome out on a field trip. Sometimes at the park she would create a treasure hunt where they were each given a list of items they were required to find. Because Cohen wasn't able to read, Gabrielle would draw miniature pictures beside the word list. That way Cohen could figure out the word all on his own, which pleased him tremendously. Each child was presented with a gunny sack and they would run noisily around the park in search of the required items.

Before the hunt began, Gabrielle always made sure to point out the boundaries of their search and made it crystal clear that they were never to disappear out of her sight. The children loved the freedom and the competition of the game.

Today wasn't Friday, but Gabrielle felt the children had seemed restless lately. Since the weather outside was warm and sunny she decided to make up an extra special treasure hunt with prizes upon completion. Gabrielle was excited! The list had a bit of a twist to it today and she wasn't sure that the children would be able to figure it out.

Hurrying off to the bus stop that took Gabrielle to the hotel where the children stayed, she found a familiar tune bee-bopping in her head. *I sure hope the children are up for this adventure,* she thought.

The bus ride lasted exactly fifteen minutes and Gabrielle pulled the bell chord to stop the bus. Hurrying into the Ritz Renaissance Hotel the doorman greeted her with a warm smile.

"Good morning, Miss Gabrielle, you look like you're in a hurry! Have a great day," he announced as she whizzed past him.

"Thank you, Mr. Weatherby, I will and you too!" Gabrielle responded without missing a beat.

Upon arriving at her destination, Gabrielle learned of the new developments and how the children wanted to spend the morning at the gym. She was disappointed. She had spent a lot of time planning the special outing in the park.

Meaghan noticed the disappointed look on Gabrielle's face and came to her rescue.

"Tara and Cohen, I know you want to come to the gym today, but I really should ask Tony about it first. He won't be expecting you and it might ruffle his feathers if we have a sudden change of plans."

"Tony doesn't have fedders!" Cohen stated, giggling at the funny thought.

"You're right Cohen, he doesn't have fedders." Meaghan laughed, mussing Cohen's dark hair. "But I should check with him first. I'll try and get him to let us all come to the gym on Friday. I think that will work out better!" Meaghan assured them, glancing over at Gabrielle to check out her reaction.

Gabrielle's face brightened and she said, "That would be wonderful. I'll plan on taking the children to the gym on Friday. I've designed a special treasure hunt for them today, across the street in the park."

"That sounds like lots of fun." Meaghan responded.

"Yay!" Both Tara and Cohen replied. "Can we go now?" Cohen asked.

"Yes we can, as soon as you go to the bathroom!"

Tara and Cohen ensued in a mini argument over who would use the bathroom first, but Sara came to the rescue, ushering Cohen into the main bathroom and Sara into the ensuite.

Once Gabrielle had guided the children across the street to the park, she gave each of them their list of required items to find: first item – toadstool or mushroom.

Cohen spied a spotted mushroom hiding in the shade of a huge sprawling tree. He sprinted over to take a closer look and then immediately called out excitedly, "Over here, I found one, come and see."

Gabrielle had taught the children that they were not to pick the mandatory item.

She and Tara ran over to inspect Cohen's find. The three were huddled together viewing the large spotted toadstool when a tall, thin, weather-beaten looking man approached them and asked if he could take a look!

Cohen silently pointed down to the mushroom, Tara and Gabrielle stood beside Cohen.

No one said a word.

"That's a mighty fine mushroom, young man, you found it very quickly!" the man said and then continued, "You don't have to be afraid of me. I have kids myself and I won't hurt you."

Gabrielle thought, *how did this stranger know Cohen found it quickly? He must have been watching us!* She took hold of Cohen's hand on one side and Tara's hand on the other side and started leading them towards the hotel.

The stranger quickly stepped up to join them and looking into Gabrielle's dark eyes, said, "Hey there, pretty girl, there's a burger joint just down the street, how about we all go there and I'll buy us some French fries and ice cream?"

Gabrielle looked the stranger in the eye and replied. "No thank you, sir, it's time for the children to get back to the hotel," and the trio continued walking away.

Marty watching his opportunity walk away began to lose his composure. He blurted out, "Not so fast, young lady. Who do ya think ya are? These are my kids and I got a right ta spend some time with them if I want to!"

Gabrielle and the children began walking faster, practically running, towards the hotel.

From the corner of her eye, Gabrielle saw the form of a woman hurrying towards them and realized it was Sara. The children spotted her and ran ahead to meet her.

Gabrielle sprinted along right behind them.

"Sara, I found a mushroom! I was the first one too. I found one afore Tara!" Cohen exclaimed.

"That's great Cohen, good for you. I'm very proud of you!" Sara replied, brushing his cheek quickly in a loving gesture with her hand and then continued. "Now I want the three of you to run along to the hotel and get inside, I will join you in a few minutes. Go on!"

"But we just got here!" Cohen wailed.

Gabrielle once again, protectively took each child's hand and said, "I know Cohen, but we'll go inside until that weird guy goes away. We can come back later. Now *hurry!*"

Sara stood her ground and turned to meet Marty face to face. "Why are you aggravating these children?"

Marty's face contorted into a sneer and he said. "Hey there lady, what's got your knickers in a knot?"

Sara looked Marty up and down disdainfully and replied, "First of all, you have no idea if I'm a lady or not and secondly – if my knickers are in a knot it's certainly none of your business." And with that Sara turned to leave.

Marty took a giant step forward, grabbing Sara by the arm. "Those are *my kids*!"

Sara paused, looked at the stranger and said in a calm menacing voice even she didn't know she possessed, "Listen mister, I have no idea who you are, and frankly I don't really care! However, I am responsible for those two beautiful children and their tutor and you will not get past me to them. These children belong to my amazing friend and employer." Raising her index finger and shoving it in Marty's face, she continued, "If you decide to hassle them in any way, you will have to deal with me and I will not hesitate to call the police."

"Aw lady, calm down. I'm not gonna hurt them. I just wanna talk to them and tell them I'm their dad." Marty said, turning on his most charming smile.

Sara took a step back and looked Marty over from his sun-bleached blond hair to his worn out, dirty, scuffed, sneakers.

Returning her gaze back up to his smiling face, Sara replied in a quiet steady voice, "If you continue to hassle me or these children in any way, I *will* call the police!" Then as if she was

Dorothy in the "Wizard of Oz" she clicked her heels together and started walking towards the hotel.

Marty watched.

Chapter 20
MORE MARTY TROUBLE

Big drops of sweat were rolling down Meaghan's face. Monday was her heaviest workout day, or maybe it just felt like it because she had the weekends off. Tony, her personal trainer undertook to get very ounce of fortitude out of her.

He had promised her that every grunt and gyration that came out of her mouth would count towards the end results.

Meaghan had a choice of trainers when she first arrived for the fitness program, but Tony won, hands down. There wasn't an inch to pinch on his firm physique and as time went on Meaghan became more and more impressed with his training style.

The personal program of exercises that Tony had provided for Meaghan and his intense pursuit of discipline helped her work through each gym day, and she was achieving her desire to look and feel her best.

Up down, up down, Meaghan was on her seventh crunch when Tony came towards her holding out his cell phone. "This call is for you!" he said, handing Meaghan the phone.

Meaghan stopped crunching and gave him a quizzical look, "For me?"

Grabbing the phone with one sweaty hand and brushing away stray stands of damp hair with the other one she put the phone to her ear and said, "Hallo!"

"Hello Meaghan, how ya been doin'?" The male voice on the other end of the line said in a deep voice. "It's me, Marty. I've been lookin' everywhere for ya. You sure know how to do a disappearin' act. I thought maybe us two could get together and have a lil ole talk. For old times' sake, what d'ya think of that?"

Meaghan pulled the phone away from her ear, looking at it as if it was contaminated. After a few seconds, she returned the phone to her ear and said in a dull monotone, "What do you want, Marty?"

"I want to see you – and my kids. They're my kids too you know. Don't you think it's about time we introduced them to their ole dad?" Marty finished with a laugh.

"I can't talk to you right now. How did you get this number? I'll call you back later. Is your cell phone number still the same?" Meaghan asked.

"It was easy to get this number, I just called the hotel and they put me through. Yeah, my number's still the same. Call me soon, sweet Meaghan, I'll be waitin'!"

Meaghan clicked off the phone and handed it back to Tony. Without saying a word she rolled over and became a plank. *What could he possibly want with us now?* She thought. *He hasn't been interested in us for over three years and now, all of a sudden he wants to see the kids?"*

Too restless to continue being a plank, Meaghan jumped up and started running. She tore around the gym in circles. *I think my brain's going in circles. What is Marty up to?*

Finally stopping to take a sip of water, she grabbed a towel and began sopping up sweat from her face and neck. She picked up a ten pound barbell in each hand and angrily started pumping them up and down. *Marty Summers,* she thought. *If you're just messing with us, you're in big trouble. You better not be playing games with me and the kids! If you want to be a part of their lives fine, but, you're not going to bounce in and out whenever it suits you. These children deserve much more than a deadbeat dad!*

"Whoah, whoever that was on the phone sure got you going. I've been trying to get you working like that all along. Can I ask whoever that was if he wants a job?" Tony asked, sidling up to Meaghan's side.

Meaghan's stress spent, she let out a little laugh and replied. "I just needed to get something out of my system. It's all gone now. I'm ready to hit the shower. Thanks Tony, you do a good job for me and I appreciate it."

"No problem, Meaghan. If something comes up that you need help with, anything at all, you know you can call on me!"

"I know Tony, thanks, I'm sure it'll be fine." Meaghan said. She gave Tony a grateful smile and raised her hand in a high five salute. They smacked hands and Meaghan headed for the shower room. "See you tomorrow, Tony."

Chapter 21
DAD OR NO DAD

Sara hurried up to Meaghan's hotel suite, anxious to learn how the children would be coping with the "Dad information." She wasn't sure she knew how to handle this chain of events! Silently praying all the way to the top floor, she trusted God would give her the right words.

Sliding her key card into the door slot, she quietly opened it and took a look around. "Where are the kids?" she asked Gabrielle, who was sitting calmly on the couch and texting.

"Oh they're sitting on their mom's bed watching a cartoon," she replied with a flip of her hand in that general direction.

"Gabrielle, have you ever seen that man we met in the park before?" Sara asked.

"Naw, he was kind of a weirdo, wasn't he? Thanks for coming to our rescue; it was kinda scary, when I think about it!" Gabrielle responded, pondering the situation.

"Yes, he was scary. I hope we never have to deal with him again. What did the children say?"

"Not too much. Tara thought he must be a man living on the street. Cohen suggested that maybe he was an alien that somehow lost his kids on another planet." Gabrielle said with a small nervous laugh, lifting her hands in bewilderment.

"Okay, well I'll go have a talk to them, you better come too. We need to keep our stories straight, whatever that will be!" Sara suggested.

"Okay, just a minute. I need to finish this message."

Sara and Gabrielle walked into the bedroom and sat down, one on each side of the bed. Sara pointed to the TV and said, "Hey guys, can I shut this off for a few minutes? I'd like to talk to you."

"Aw," Cohen said, "That's my favrit show!"

"Just for a couple of minutes," Sara responded.

The children nodded and Tara said "I don't like this show anyway, it's for babies."

Sara picked up the remote and clicked the TV off. When she had everyone's full attention Sara asked, "Does anybody know that man who talked to us in the park today?"

Tara shook her head no and Cohen said gravely, "He thinks we're his kids. Maybe he lost his kids."

"Maybe he did!" Sara said. "I don't know that man either. We'll talk to your mother about it when she gets home. But I don't want anybody to worry about it.

We're all safe and I'm sure that man is long gone by now. Did you finish your school work for this morning?

The children both started shouting about how they were working on a treasure hunt in the park when "that man" interrupted them.

"Why don't I fix you treasure hunters an amazing snack and Gabrielle will think of a special game to play inside today. Do either of you have any ideas?" Sara asked.

"Cookies," shouted Cohen, "I wanna cookie!"

"Chips," exclaimed Tara. "Let's have chips!"

"I meant ideas about an amazing activity not an amazing snack," Sara said with a chuckle. "I'll see what I can find." She left the room. *Children,* she thought, *they have no worries and a great knack for living in the present, we should be more like them. What's done is done, let's move on.*

Making her way into the kitchen, Sara thought, *I wonder what that man was up to. I'm anxious to hear what Meaghan thinks about it!*

Chapter 22
LEAVING VANCOUVER

"Meaghan," Cassandra, the Enlighten Weight Loss CEO ambled up to her side, while calling out her name.

Meaghan swung around with a questioning look on her face. "Yes?"

"We're going to be leaving Vancouver later this week. I don't know if anyone has officially told you yet."

"No, not really, I heard some rumblings from Tony, but no one has formally told me," she answered.

"Well consider this your official notification," Cassandra replied with a sweet smile. "Vancouver has been very good for us, and you have been very good for Vancouver, Meaghan, but it's time to move on! I believe we've done all we can do here."

"Edmonton's our next city right?" Meaghan had mixed feelings about this decision. If there was one thing that was a drawback with the Enlighten Weight Loss company it was that she had no control over where she would be and for how long! The first leg of their journey in Vancouver had been a great success. The Enlighten Program had opened up fourteen new offices in centres throughout Vancouver and surrounding area, with a total of over seven hundred and fifty new members signing up for the weight loss program. The company had received only positive feedback regarding the program and continued to believe that it was a much needed service.

People of all cultures and backgrounds were shedding pounds and Meaghan was doing her best to be a definitive role model everyone could relate to. She loved her work and was finding it hard to imagine doing anything else, but it wasn't all glamour, she worked hard to keep physically fit and always show a happy disposition.

Taking the elevator up to her room for lunch, Meaghan was imagining what the kids would be doing this morning. *Gabrielle's taking them to the park. I wonder how that's going. I'm sure they're having fun!*

Meaghan opened the door and was surprised to see Sara, Gabrielle, Tara and Cohen all inside sitting around the table. "What's going on here?" she asked, reaching out to hug her children.

"We're having a snack!" Cohen announced.

"I see that!" Meaghan responded. "How come you're not outside, playing at the park?"

Tara looked up at her mother, a serious expression on her face as she told her. "There was a strange man at the park and he was bothering us. He called me and Cohen *his kids!*" She emphasized the words his kids, as if to say, "Can you imagine that?"

Meaghan was horrified and looked from Sara to Gabrielle, "Is this true?"

Gabrielle replied. "Yes, he wanted to buy us fries and ice cream. When we refused, he started to go a little berserk! He accused me of keeping him from his kids!"

"Well that's weird! I wonder what his problem is. Did he do or say anything else?" Meaghan asked.

At this point Sara chimed in, "I was coming out of our hotel when I saw a strange man talking to Gabrielle and the kids so I rushed over and to help Gaby get everyone inside the hotel. I'm not sure what it was all about. He must be emotionally unstable!"

Could that have been Marty? Meaghan thought, but said out loud, "That's very strange! It sounds like you did the right thing by getting the children away from him and inside the hotel! Thank you, Gaby and Sara." Meaghan directed a smile at each of them.

"And you two munchkins, good job listening and staying safe. This is a big city and I sure don't want anything bad to happen to you." Meaghan assured them.

Just then Gabrielle came up with an amazing idea, "Hey you two, I've got a new idea for our field trip. I know the swimming pool is available at this time of day. Let's go downstairs for a swim. I'm going to count how many laps each of you can do!"

"Yay, swimming!" the children shouted.

"Let's *go!*" Tara said, flashing a smile at her mother. The threesome left the room to get their swimming gear on.

Sara looked thoughtfully at Meaghan and asked. "Do you have any ideas about the strange man?"

"Yes, I most certainly do," Meaghan answered, in a hushed voice. "I'll tell you about it once I know the kids are out of earshot."

When they heard the front door close with a click and she was positive that the children and Gabrielle were gone, Meaghan told Sara about Marty contacting her.

"All of a sudden, out of the blue he thinks he wants to be a part of our family. I'm not sure why! He couldn't wait to get me out of his life the last time I saw him!"

Chapter 23

ANNA AND SILK

Anna and her husband Silk were relaxing on thick, peony red, overly stuffed lounge chairs in the backyard of their close friends Kent and Irene's comfortable home in Saskatoon. Their friends were away on a vacation to Costa Rica so when they heard that Anna and Silk would be in the city for several weeks they immediately offered them the use of their home.

The air felt quite cool outside, but Anna felt the need to breathe in some invigorating fresh air. Reclined in the padded chair, Silk had bundled her up in a thick wool blanket; she was feeling very comfortable and loved.

After undergoing her third round of chemotherapy, Anna realized the chemicals were beginning to take their toll on her energy and endurance, or was it the cancer? Anna really didn't know, she would ask her doctor!

"You're doing great, Anna." Silk told her in his soft husky voice. "Only three more treatments and then you get to take a break! We are going to beat this disease, with God's help, and then the two of us are going to take a nice long vacation, somewhere hot, with a beach."

Anna looked lovingly at Silk.

"That sounds very nice Silk. You're always so positive, what would I do without you?"

"Well young lady, that is something you will never know, because I will always be here to take care of you, so don't even think about it!" Silk replied.

Recently Anna's breast cancer had metastasized with a vengeance to lymph nodes under her arms, and her oncology doctors decided to change her treatment from radiation to chemotherapy.

Of course, this news had been heartbreaking to Anna and Silk and their family. Everyone had been so certain that the cancer wouldn't come back after the first round of radiation. Their daughter, Cindy, was devastated when her dad called her with the news. She desperately wanted to come to Saskatoon and take care of her mother, but Anna convinced her to wait until all the chemo treatments were finished and then they could all go home where it would be more comfortable.

Anna knew that the powerful drugs would knock her out and she'd be sleeping most of the time anyway. She wanted her daughter to be there for her when she would be more alert and able to enjoy their time together.

Anna missed Cindy. The two of them had a very close connection. They laughed at the same jokes, liked the same kind of foods and enjoyed the same movies.

"Maybe we can rent some movies when Cindy comes for her visit," Anna thought out loud.

"What did you say?" Silk asked.

"I was just thinking that when Cindy comes for her visit, I'd like to watch some movies with her," Anna replied.

"I think that's a great idea, I know you two love watching movies together!" Silk replied with a smile at his wife. They both knew this was a battle for Anna's life.

Silk had called upon their church family to pray for Anna and he knew that the members were faithfully doing so at numerous prayer meetings and individually. The couple themselves had undertaken to fast and pray.

One of Anna's favourite Bible stories was Esther. A single Jewish woman, Esther chose to fast from food while praying for her people, the Jews. God answered Esther's prayers and gave her exceedingly more than she had requested.

Besides saving the Jewish people – from extinction, the king ordered Haman, the diabolical instigator of the decree to annihilate the Jews, to be hung on the gallows until death and Esther's own dear adopted father, Mordecai to be made administrator to the King. Esther married the King and became the reigning queen.

A few years earlier, Silk had undergone a series of minor skin cancer surgeries. Over the course of three or four years malignant cells seemed to pop up on any sun exposed skin – face, arms, and ears, forcing Silk to take the time to get the area removed by a surgeon. For each occurrence Anna chose to fast and pray that he would not sustain any continuous or serious side effects from the cancer. Silk was now and had been cancer free for five years.

Anna's parents had both passed from cancer. Her mother, Inga's cancer, had begun the same way as Anna's. Inga's doctors had removed both of her breasts upon the first detection of malignant cells. She had been about the same age as Anna was now. Anna remembers it seemed to work for a few years but eventually it came back more aggressively than before and ultimately Inga had no choice, the cancer took her life.

Anna's dad, Hans outlasted his loving wife by ten years. Hans had been diagnosed with prostate cancer shortly after Inga's passing but he continued to enjoy his life, as best he could without his soul mate. He spent many happy hours with his grandchildren, taking them fishing and playing softball with them. Near the end of his time, he took up the sport of playing golf, which he enjoyed tremendously until he was too sick to continue. His golfing buddies became his very good friends and a big part of his life. They filled in many long afternoons with him, playing crib or rummy.

Anna's mind snapped back to reality amid the silence and tranquility of the backyard when Silk asked her, "Can I get you anything?"

"No, I'm fine, just relax. It really is beautiful and peaceful out here. I'm glad we came outside. I can barely hear the traffic. Can you?"

"No, it's nice and quiet, honey. But if you start getting cold you let me know and we'll get you inside. The air is really starting to cool off."

Anna chuckled, "You think I'm going to get cold wrapped up like this? I might stay out here all night."

"I'm glad you're feeling nice and cozy, but I know I can't make it out here all night, so don't go getting any funny ideas." Silk warned her with a smile.

Chapter 24
LUC AND LISA

Luc arrived at his hotel in Saskatoon after an uneventful flight from Vancouver. Lisa had requested Luc to meet her at the Red Lion Bar and Grill at 8:00 p.m.

He hailed a cab outside his hotel room and absently-mindedly asked the taxi driver to take him to the Red Lion Bar and Grill. Upon arrival he reached into his jeans pocket and pulled out some bills to pay the driver.

Luc had been feeling apprehensive all day about meeting up with his ex-girlfriend, Lisa, but he knew it was something he had to do – he wanted to save this child – even if it meant getting together with Lisa.

Walking into the dimly lit bar, it took a moment for Luc's eyes to adjust.

Then he spotted her. He stopped and stared for a few seconds at a solitary figure sitting in a shadowy corner booth. Knowing this meeting could change his life forever, Luc sent up a silent prayer, asking God to guide his thoughts and words.

Lisa is a good person, he thought. *I know now that she's not the right girl for me, but if I hadn't met Meaghan I may very well have hooked up with her and maybe we would have been happy together!*

Luc started moving forward as Lisa looked up and noticed him coming. She smiled and Luc remembered how beautiful she was. Walking up to her chair he leaned over and planted a silent peck on her cheek.

"Hello, Lisa," he said with a warm smile. "How are you?"

"Hi Luc," Lisa replied. "I'm doing okay. You know there are still two of us here, and today we are both feeling fine!" Rubbing her tummy, she continued "Sometimes it feels like this little guy is doing somersaults, but he must be taking a break at the moment, all is calm. Sit down Luc. I want to tell you all about us."

Luc did just that. He pulled out the chair beside Lisa and gave her his full attention. "Tell me," he said. "I'm all ears!"

Just then their drink waiter appeared and introduced himself as Carlos. Luc ordered a glass of Merlot and Lisa requested iced tea. Carlos gave them an exaggerated bow and told them he would be right back.

"I've given up alcohol completely, for now," Lisa told Luc with a little smile.

"Good for you, I'm proud of you. Sounds like you are taking good care of your baby," Luc replied.

"I'm trying. I'm starting to feel attached to this little guy. I didn't think I would but my feelings are changing."

Just then Carlos reappeared, drinks in hand and the couple each ordered an aperitif.

Luc began to relax. He had called his mother earlier that day and asked her to pray for them. Not being sure what Lisa's expectations were, he knew he needed wisdom to get him through the evening. Slowly, cautiously, Lisa told Luc little anecdotes about her changing lifestyle.

Luc's heart filled with compassion as she told him how the first couple of months involved a lot of morning sickness, requiring her to pretty much stay at home as her so-called "morning" sickness, could come on any time of the day.

"But thankfully, that phase of my pregnancy is over and now I'm feeling healthy and strong," Lisa continued and then looking up into Luc's eyes asked, "Luc, do you still want to marry me?"

Just then Carlos returned with the appetizers and carefully placed them before the couple. After Luc thanked him, Carlos once again performed his exaggerated bow and hurried away.

Luc thought for a moment and then answered her question with a question of his own. "Lisa, does my answer affect the outcome of this baby's life?"

Lisa's gaze never wavered, "Well, actually it does affect the outcome of the baby's life. But not how you think. I'm not going to get an abortion. It's too late for that. At first I didn't want anything to do with this baby – you know that. I didn't even appreciate what a good man you are to offer to marry me and raise this baby together, as a family. But now, if you no longer have the desire to marry me then I want to give the baby to you, Luc. I'm not willing to make the sacrifice to be a single parent. I might want to have some involvement in the baby's life – or I might not! I don't know yet."

A jolt of adrenalin rushed through Luc's body as his mind registered what Lisa was saying! He felt as if he'd been struck by lightning. Gathering his thoughts, he calmly asked, "Lisa, do you love me?"

Lisa studied Luc's face for what seemed like ages to Luc. Then looking down at her hands twisted together in her lap, she replied, "I don't love you Luc. I want to! I know you are probably the best, kindest man I've ever dated, and I know you will make a great father to this baby, but I haven't been missing you the way I should if I were head over heels in love with you."

Luc let out his breath, not realizing he'd been holding it. Once more he smiled at Lisa and said, "Thanks for being honest, Lisa."

Luc was still trying to wrap his mind around the news Lisa had just shared with him, *she doesn't want the baby but wants me to have it! That's crazy!* Voicing his thoughts he asked, "Are you sure you don't want to keep this baby? You might change your mind after it's born."

Lisa quickly answered, "No Luc, I've made an appointment for us to see a lawyer tomorrow, at ten o'clock. Her office is close to here, it's the Burlingham Law Office.

Does that time work for you? You're not working in the morning right?" Lisa quickly rushed on. "I've asked her to draw up the papers giving you full custody of this child, but," she looked shyly up at Luc, "I do want a clause in there allowing me visiting rights if at some point I feel that I want to exercise that right. Can you live with that?"

"Of course I can, Lisa. If you have the desire to know this child then I will make sure you have that right. But are you really sure this is what you want?"

"Yes. I've given this much thought. You will be the best parent for this child!" Pausing, she added with finality, "That's settled then. We will take care of all the paperwork in the morning. Thank you Luc, your kindness means a lot to me. You are a good man, and I know our baby will be in good hands," Lisa said covering Luc's big hand with her own tiny one.

"So when is this little one going to make its appearance?"

Chapter 25

A REAL DAD

"In about four more months, that will be early December. The doctor predicts December 10th!" Lisa replied.

The couple made small talk while they nibbled on their food. Luc's stomach was doing nervous flip-flops, as he thought of the role as a father that had just been handed to him.

Lisa was silently breathing a sigh of relief. She had met someone new and was ready to get on with that relationship. She wasn't sure that he would be the right partner for her either but she longed for someone to share her life with and felt that giving Luc the baby was absolutely the best solution to the situation. It was as if a huge weight had been lifted from her shoulders and she had a hard time holding back her gratitude.

Riding back to his hotel room, Luc was feeling ecstatic. He was going to be a *real* dad. He couldn't wait to share the news with Meaghan and his mom, but decided he would wait to tell them until after the visit with the lawyer. He knew Lisa well enough to know that she was prone to mind changes!

He would have to think of names! *I never thought to ask Lisa. I wonder if she knows if it's a boy or a girl. She did keep referring to the baby as "he" I wonder if that means anything?*

With that thought in mind, the taxi came to a stop and Luc jumped out at his destination. After paying the driver he decided to go for a long walk.

Life was good and getting better by the moment. "Thank You God!"

Chapter 26

THREE MONTHS LATER – FALLING IN LOVE

Once again Meaghan and Luc were out on a date, this time at the Riverside Lounge in Saskatoon, Saskatchewan.

The last couple of months had been an idyllic love story for Luc and Meaghan. Amidst the transitions, first from Vancouver, to Edmonton, and then six weeks later to Saskatoon, the couple found themselves becoming very amiable.

At first the move to Edmonton had put a big bump in the road of their relationship, but intermittently Luc managed to wangle an overnight flight with a stopover in Edmonton and they made the most of this opportunity for an evening out together. On his days off, Luc sometimes would catch a flight to Edmonton and spend his time with Meaghan, her children, and his mother of course. The couple came to realize that they were falling deeply in love with each other.

Finally, the special night came: Luc planned on proposing marriage to Meaghan.

His mother's engagement ring was safely secured in a zippered pocket in his wallet, which he nervously kept pushing into his back pocket. He wanted to make sure it was still there.

Their date began with Meaghan looking radiant, as usual, and Luc couldn't take his eyes off her. Her long, dark glistening hair hung loosely down her back and her beautiful hazel eyes sparkled with happiness.

Sara was once again looking after Tara and Cohen. Luc had made her privy to the proposal plan and she was delighted. She couldn't think of anyone she would rather have for a daughter-in-law or anyone who would make Luc a more loving wife. Of course the bonus for both of them was Meaghan's children, who had already begun calling her Gramma Sara.

The music began playing a slow easy waltz and Luc asked Meaghan if she would like to dance. Meaghan was thrilled. "Of course, I would love to dance with you!"

Luc wrapped both his arms around Meaghan, she smiled up at him and slipped her arms up and around his neck. "This is beautiful!" she murmured.

"Yes, I agree, this is exactly where I want to be. You are beautiful, Meaghan!" Luc replied.

Meaghan looked up at Luc with a look of scepticism on her face.

"Didn't anyone ever tell you that you're beautiful?' he asked.

"You know Luc, certain people throughout my life have told me I'm beautiful, or I'm special and then for whatever reason they've treated me badly. So now it seems I have very little faith in words. If I'm so beautiful or if I'm so special, why don't they treat me accordingly? I've decided that I'll take action rather than words any day. Words are just words. Does that make any sense to you?"

"It makes perfect sense to me. Thank you for sharing that with me."

They swayed slowly to the music. When it ended Luc took a step back and reached out for both of Meaghan's hands. In a voice husky with emotion he said, "Meaghan, I want to ask you something!"

"What is it, Luc? Is something wrong?"

"No Meaghan, everything is absolutely right. Do you have any idea how happy you make me?"

Meaghan looked steadily into Luc's deep brown eyes and said, "You know I feel exactly the same way. When I'm with you I feel a deep sense of peace, it's like I'm right where I belong."

"Well that makes my next question less nerve-wracking then," Luc continued with a nervous chuckle. Not being able to wait a second longer, he looked deeply into Meaghan's eyes, and in a voice full of emotion he said, "Meaghan, I would be honoured if you would become my wife. Will you marry me?"

Meaghan looked back at Luc. "What did you just say?" she asked. Meaghan had been hoping this would happen and was pretty sure it was going to – sooner or later, but she couldn't believe the moment had arrived. Her mouth dropped open and she stared at Luc.

"Well, are you?" he continued.

Letting out a little squeal, she stepped up on her tippy toes, and gave Luc a tender kiss smack on his mouth. "*Yes, yes, yes*, I will marry you!"

At that moment the band started playing, *Can I have this Dance for the Rest of My Life?* By Anne Murray and the ecstatic couple, wrapped in each other's arms sang the song to each other, oblivious to the pleasing looks that the other patrons were casting in their direction.

"Can I have this dance for the rest of my life?

Will you be my partner every night?

When we're together it feels so right, Can I have this dance for the rest of my life?"

Chapter 27
WHAT'S IN A NAME?

Luc, Tara and Cohen were taking a leisurely walk along a winding pathway beside the South Saskatchewan River.

"Oh look, there's some ducks swimming over there!" Luc said, pointing a ways down the river.

"I like ducks!" Cohen stated matter-of-factly.

They walked a few more metres and then came upon a stone bench.

"Let's sit here for a while – take a break," Luc said. He pulled out brightly colored water bottles from his back pack and passed them around. "Orange one for Tara, green one for Cohen and I get the blue one." After taking a big drink, he brought up the subject of "the baby."

Meaghan and Luc had told the children they would be getting married soon and a new baby would be in their lives presently, but the children weren't sure of the details. Meaghan wanted Luc to tell them the whole story.

"The new baby is going to be a little girl!" Luc stated.

"How do you know that? Did she get born already?" Tara asked in an accusing voice.

"No, she's not born yet, but the doctor took a picture of the mother's tummy, and the picture showed a baby girl inside," Luc answered.

"I want a boy!" Cohen stated.

"I know you do Cohen, but it's a girl and we can't change that," Luc said ruffling Cohen's hair. "I think a girl will be okay, but we need to think of a good name for her. Can anyone think of a beautiful name for a baby girl?"

Tara sat back deep in thought.

Cohen piped up, "I think we should call her Luc, after you."

Luc laughed. "I don't think Luc is a girl's name, but maybe Lucy, what do you think of that name, Cohen?"

"Yeah, Lucy, I like that. That's a good name for a girl." The matter was settled as far as Cohen was concerned and he raced off to chase a brightly colored butterfly.

"Don't go far!" Luc cautioned.

"I won't!" Cohen replied, still chasing the beautiful Monarch butterfly.

"What do you think Tara? Are you happy the baby's a little girl? Can you think of any good names?" Luc asked, slipping his arm around Tara's small shoulders.

"Yes, I'm happy it's going to be a girl!" Tara replied seriously. "I can think of lots of great names: Kierra, Madison, Noelle, Charlotte, Sofie, Tamzen, Faith, Taylor, or what about Sara like your mom?" Tara asked, stopping to catch her breath.

Luc let out a laugh and said, "That is a lot of great names, Tara. Do you have any more?"

"Those are my favourites right now, but if I think of anymore I'll let you know."

"Well I will appreciate that, Tara. You know the baby will be here soon so we need to have a name ready, and we can't use all your favourites. Is there one special name?"

"Today my favourite is Kierra, but Cohen wants the baby named Lucy, how will you decide?" Tara asked.

Luc was enjoying the conversation with Tara immensely, "I can see that it will be a tough decision. You know that since

I'm going to be marrying your mother this baby will be your little sister?"

"Really?" Tara asked, jumping up from the bench and facing Luc. "How long will she be living with us?"

"Yes really!" Luc promised. "She will always live with us, just like you and Cohen, until she's grown up!"

Tara reached out, wrapped her arms around Luc's neck and said, "That makes me so happy – a new baby sister! You know Luc, whatever name you choose is okay with me. I like the name Lucy too. Does Cohen know this will be our sister? I better go tell him."

She raced off to catch up with her little brother and Luc felt overwhelmed with the enormous blessings that were becoming part of his life – the woman he adored would soon be his wife, Tara and Cohen would be his children and soon a brand new baby daughter.

"Thank you, Lord," he said, "I can't imagine life getting any better than this!"

Chapter 28

MARTY SINGS THE BLUES

Marty was precariously perched on a barstool at the Sundown Bar in Saskatoon for his last drink of the night.

Following Meaghan around for the last three months was beginning to take its toll. He was happy to be back in Saskatoon, he knew the territory and living here was a lot cheaper than living in Vancouver or Edmonton. *It's good to be home,* he thought.

"But my sweet Meaghan's gettin' married to some big shot airline pilot, what's a guy supposed to do? I tried my best to win her back. Beggin' and pleadin's not really my bag, I told her that. I even kicked my live-in girlfriend, Amber and her little brat outta my life." Marty remembered one not so sober telephone call when he told Meaghan he was gonna steal the kids if she didn't come back to him. Meaghan wouldn't budge. And now this, he ran his hand through his hair. "I need to come up with a new plan!"

He slugged back a shot of straight whiskey. "Why is life so unfair, just when I catch up to Meaghan and the kids again they're makin' other plans? Maybe I need to have a little visit with that fiancé of hers. She probly never even told him 'bout me. I bet he doesn't know she's already got a husband!"

The bartender shouted at him above the din in the room. "Wanna 'nother one?"

"I can't afford any more of this crap. Bring me a beer!" Marty slurred.

The bartender, a seasoned veteran in the bartending business produced a beer mug with foam overflowing down the sides. Slamming it on the counter in front of Marty, he asked, "You got troubles, mister?"

"Yeah, you could say that – my wife's runnin off and marryin' up with some big shot airline pilot!"

"How can she be your wife then?" the bartender asked.

"Well, she's my ex, but I been trying to get her back. She's got it made on easy street, parading around in fancy clothes, bringin' in the big money. She sure forgets about her old man when she gets important," Marty whined.

"And what do you do fer a living?" the bartender asked.

"I'm kinda in between jobs right now. I do construction work, but it's been real slow and I got laid off. I been livin' with a woman who's got a snotty nose kid; she kept me in beer money, maybe I better get her back," Marty volunteered.

"Sounds like you're the one who's got it made – runnin' after women, them taking care of you, sittin in the bar drinking, you got a pretty good life if you ask me," the bartender suggested.

"Yeah, I guess it could be worse all right. I just don't know how long I can put up with that bawlin' brat of hers. He's always makin' a racket over something! But guess I can't follow sweet Meaghan around for the rest of my life. She's threatnin' to get a restrainin' order against me if I keep pesterin' her and the kids. Maybe I should start lookin' for a new little sweet thing to take care of ole Marty." He swivelled around on his bar stool, "Any prospects in here, any pretty little ladies lookin' for a strong, handsome, available man?"

The bartender shook his head, he'd seen all kinds in his job, but this guy was right up there with the worst – no job – no respect for women – it was all about him. He looked at Marty and said, "Don't see anyone looking around for a man right now, but if something comes up, I'll be sure to let you know!"

Marty continued, "Whatever, I'm not gonna waste any more time chasin' after Meaghan. She wants to be a hot shot pilot's wife then I'm done with her. There's more fish in the sea than the Mighty Meaghan and she's not gettin' any child support outta me anyway so I'm free to move on." Marty took a big swig of beer and rubbed the back of his hand over his mouth to catch the foam.

The bartender studied Marty for a few seconds, thinking, *the bottle's gonna get him. I wonder why some people trade in their life for a bottle? Guess I shouldn't complain, it keeps me in business, but I see too much of this junk – guys leaving their wives and families, making bad choices all because of alcohol.*

Marty swigged down the last of his beer, threw some money on the counter and wobbled out of the bar. *That's it,* he thought, *I'm done with Meaghan, I'll put up with Amber and her whiny kid for now, until somethin' better comes along!*

Chapter 29
I DO I DO I DO

Meaghan waited at the back of the flower filled chapel basking in the wonderful blessedness of this special day. In a few moments, she would be walking down the aisle to be united with the most kind, caring, loving man she had ever met. Her adorable, excited children would be walking with her, one on each side. Meaghan's beautiful face was beaming. Dressed in an ankle length simple, silk ivory wraparound dress, Meaghan looked absolutely stunning. Her long, shimmering, black hair hung loosely down her back with the front pinned to the side with a miniature deep pink peony. She carried no bouquet, leaving that task to Tara who was carrying a small white wicker basket overflowing with rose pink carnation petals. Cohen proudly clutched the bridal couple's matching wedding bands attached to a delicate silver pillow.

Tara was trying very hard not to bounce. Her excitement was overwhelming! She loved the new sparkly sky blue, organza dress her mother had chosen for her and the new white pearl patent leather shoes had a bit of a high heel making her feel very grown up.

After all, she would soon be turning seven. In her mind she was practically a teenager! She found it hard not to look down and check out her shoes as she walked. Tara's long white blonde hair was left hanging loosely on her shoulders in the same style as her mother's. The front was pinned to the side with two tiny pink carnations keeping it from falling into her pretty face.

Three-year-old Cohen was dressed identical to Luc and he too was very excited. Luc was going to be his dad!

He wore a size three dove grey tuxedo with charcoal grey silk trim and a black velvet bowtie. Underneath, he was wearing a white silk shirt. Pinned to his lapel was a tiny pink carnation boutonniere. His feet proudly sported black alligator oxfords. He insisted that because today was a special day he should get to have hair gel in his hair and then had taken a brush and brushed his dark hair until it stood straight up. "There!" he exclaimed when done. He looked absolutely adorable as he waited to walk down the aisle beside his mother and sister.

The children had both been warned that this day was very important to their mom and Luc and that the church part of the day had to be very serious, Tara and Cohen were playing their role accordingly.

The bridal march began to play and Meaghan was pleasantly surprised as her children began walking solemnly beside her – they had been bouncing with excitement all morning and Meaghan had to admit that she felt like bouncing as well. Earlier Tara and Cohen had made up a little rhyme which they had sung repeatedly, "Luc's going to be our dad, and we are glad!"

As much as Meaghan wasn't prepared to fall in love again, she had done exactly that. She had fallen deeply and passionately in love with Luc and she felt certain that he was feeling exactly the same way about her.

Strolling slowly down the aisle, she looked up and straight into the deep brown eyes of the man she would spend the rest of her life with. His eyes were overflowing with love for her. Tears were running down his cheeks. Meaghan felt blessed. "Thank you, God!" she whispered.

When Meaghan and her children arrived at the front of the chapel, the mother of the groom elegantly dressed in a beautiful full skirted indigo silk two piece suit stood up and took Tara and Cohen by their hands. She smiled gently at each one and then led them to their seats beside her in the front row of the church. They sat down.

Luc took hold of Meaghan's hands in his and they stood facing each other in front of the pastor. The pastor prayed and then began the wedding service. "Dearly beloved, we are gathered here together in the sight of God and man to join these two people together in holy matrimony. If anyone here objects to these two being united I ask them to speak now or forever hold their peace."

The room was silent. Luc was then asked to proclaim the wedding vows he had prepared for Meaghan.

Luc looked solemnly into Meaghan's hazel eyes and began, "Meaghan I promise to love you and care for you, and I will try to be worthy of your love for me. I will be honest, kind, patient, forgiving and loyal to you. I promise to be your friend and a father to your children and any children we may have in the future. I promise to love you as Jesus Christ commanded us to do:

Love suffers long and is kind; love does not envy – love does not parade itself – is not puffed up – does not behave rudely. Love does not seek its own – is not provoked – thinks no evil; rejoices in the truth – bears all things – believes all things – hopes all things – endures all things. Love never fails.

Luc finished his vows with more tears streaming down his cheeks. His words touched Meaghan's soul and she was completely overwhelmed. Reaching up with soft fingertips she gently wiped the wet away.

After a few seconds of silence, the pastor asked Meaghan to recite her vows to Luc.

She began, "Luc, I promise to love you, honour you and obey you. I promise to be your friend, your lover and your partner in marriage and in parenthood. I promise to love you in sickness and in health and to be supportive of your goals and dreams.

"I feel blessed to be able to give you my hand and my heart. With God's help I will try to be the best I can be for you. I will believe in you, the person you are now, the man you will grow to be and the couple we will be together. I promise to be supportive and to always make our family's love and happiness my priority. I will dream with you, celebrate with you and walk beside you through whatever our lives may bring. You are my love today and always!"

Luc was deeply touched by Meaghan's words and he leaned over and kissed Meaghan on her yielding lips.

The pastor, looking on with reproach, warned them, "Whoah, hold on, we're not there yet!"

Luc and Meaghan exchanged a nervous smile.

The pastor continued, "Luc William Hudson do you take Meaghan Marie Marshall to be your lawfully wedded wife? If so, answer 'I do.'"

Clutching onto Meaghan's hands tightly, Luc solemnly replied, "I do."

"Meaghan Marie Marshall, do you take Luc William Hudson to be your lawfully wedded husband? If so answer 'I do.'"

Meaghan's eyes locked into Luc's and she replied, "I do."

The pastor continued, "By the power vested in me by the province of Saskatchewan, I now pronounce you husband and wife! *Now,* you may kiss the bride."

Luc wrapped his arms around Meaghan and pulled her close. He went in for a long slow kiss that took her breath away. Tara, Cohen, and Sara hurried up to the front of the church to join them.

The newly-married couple turned around to face the onrush of family and friends.

Luc's older sister, Jaycee with her husband Chad along with their twins Sol and Sammy hurried up to stand beside Sara and pass on their good wishes to the newly married couple. Luc's little brother Larry, his wife Nicole with their beautiful baby Sierra Jane had flown in to Saskatoon early that morning and made it to the church on time.

Meaghan's only family, her sister Hattie and husband Harry being from Saskatoon had been a great help and support for Meaghan in preparing for the big day. Hattie and Harry were very excited to get to know their new brother-in-law and were thrilled that Meaghan and Luc had asked them to be the official witnesses for their special day. They felt very honoured.

When Tara had met up with Aunt Hattie and Uncle Harry six weeks earlier at the airport she was full of questions about her kitten. "Did you bring Bibbs with you? Is Bibbs here? When can I see Bibbs?"

Hattie and Harry had been entrusted to care for Tara's kitten, Bibbs, also known as Snowball, while Meaghan was travelling with the children.

Aunt Hattie was happy to report to Tara that Bibbs was happily relaxing at their home but had not come to the airport to see them.

Tara was thrilled. She missed her mischievous little kitten so much and could hardly wait until she got to see her again!

The weather for this beautiful November thirtieth day of celebration of love was filled with sunshine.

Luc had organized a dinner party at the Park Place Hotel overlooking the Saskatchewan River and rented limousines were waiting outside the chapel to drive everyone to the reception. "What a thoughtful touch Luc," Meaghan told him as they were being stylishly transferred to the Park Place Hotel.

"I thought it would be easier this way since most of the family has flown in and need transportation, and then there's always the problem of parking downtown," he assured his new wife.

The limousine parade pulled up to the main entrance of the Park Place Hotel. The guests climbed out of the elegant transportation and filed into the festively decorated dining room.

Cohen and Tara and Sol and Sammy were excited to get to know each other. Baby Sierra Jane was a little too young to get involved in the antics of the other four, but she giggled on the sidelines beside her parents.

Meaghan was thrilled to finally be meeting Luc's sister and brother and their families. Champagne was served, toasts were given, and all this followed by a wonderful meal of roast venison, roasted baby potatoes, rich brown gravy, salads and side dishes.

Luc had appointed his brother Larry to be the Master of Ceremonies and Larry had lots of hilarious stories to share about Luc from his younger days. Little brother Larry had quite a sense of humour and he kept the guests in stitches throughout the meal. Some of the stories may have had a grain of truth in them but Larry had added a heap of witty embellishments.

Meaghan and Luc relaxed and thoroughly enjoyed the celebration. Their families seemed to be melding together which made for a calm delightful day.

"What a fantastic, glorious day!" Meaghan said with a sigh after finishing her last bite of raspberry filled, white chocolate cream wedding cake.

Tara, Cohen, Sol and Sammy had been recruited to help the servers pass out the delicious dessert and occasionally their fingers had "accidentally" poked into the frosting. Then, of course the fingers had to be cleaned off and what better way than a swift silent lick? The children thought this was great fun and no one told them any differently.

The evening was winding up and had officially come to a close when Luc heard his cell phone ringing. He reached into his pocket to retrieve it while apologizing to Meaghan. He pressed the answer button.

"Is this Luc Hudson?" a female voice on the other end of the line asked.

"Yes, this is Luc Hudson," he responded.

"This is Nurse Marjorie at St. Peter's Hospital. Lisa asked me to call you and tell you that she is minutes away from having your baby!"

Luc pulled the tiny phone away from his ear and looked at it, then returning it to his ear said, "Are you serious? I thought she wasn't due for another week or more! She told me December 10th!"

"Well, due date or not this baby is coming today and Lisa thought you might want to be here to see your baby being born!" the nurse continued.

"Thank you, of course, thanks for phoning, Nurse Marjorie!" Luc replied and clicked off the phone. Feeling apprehensive

– this was Meaghan's wedding day – he turned to Meaghan and blurted out that they were having a baby.

Her eyes lit up, "Well let's go see our new baby!"

Luc felt like his heart would burst with all the love he felt for his new wife. On *her* wedding day, she was full of grace and love and acceptance in welcoming his baby with another woman. *I am the luckiest man in the world,* he thought. *Meaghan is truly as beautiful on the inside as she is on the outside!*

Meaghan and Luc hurried over to Sara, who was talking to Jaycee and told them the news.

Sara wasn't sure how to respond. "Are you going to the hospital?" she asked.

"Oh yes, Sara if you don't mind. I know that would leave you with all the guests and taking care of the children – again – but if you don't mind, we do want to go and meet our new daughter," Meaghan replied.

"The evening's winding down here anyway, you two go ahead and I'll help Mom take care of Cohen and Tara!" Jaycee responded with a smile. "The children are staying with us tonight anyway, right?"

"Yes, of course, go on," Sara said pushing them towards the door.

"I need to talk to Tara and Cohen first, just a minute!" Meaghan said and the newly-married couple hurried over to talk to them. They knelt down on the floor beside Cohen and motioned for Tara to come and join them.

"Tara and Cohen," Luc started. "Your baby sister is being delivered at the hospital soon and your mom and I are going to go and meet her."

"Who is delivering her?" Tara asked. "Does she come in the courier?"

Luc and Meaghan looked at each other and exchanged a faint smile.

"It can't be Santy Clause, 'cause it's not Christmas yet!" Cohen stated, his little brow furrowing with thought.

Luc reached out and wrapped his arms around both children, "A doctor is delivering your baby sister at St. Peter's Hospital.

Perhaps another time we can explain how it all works, but not now. Your mom and I will be back as soon as we can. You stay here and have fun with Gramma Sara and your cousins."

"I want to come too!" Tara wailed.

"Not this time. We don't know how long it will take and it's very boring waiting at hospitals. You'll have more fun here," Meaghan cajoled.

She gave each of her children a quick hug and a big smooch and told them to be good.

Luc grabbed a spoon and clanked it loudly on the wooden table in order to get everyone's attention.

"Our dear families," he began, "it seems the excitement just goes on and on today. We've just received a call from the hospital and our new daughter Lucy Charlotte is coming into the world right now, so Meaghan and I are going to leave. We want to thank you all very much for coming and sharing this joy filled day with us.

"Reverend Peterson, special thanks to you for performing the beautiful service.

Now, we must run. I hope we get to see you all later."

Giving Meaghan an encompassing smile he grabbed her hand and they headed out the door to the sound of cheering and clapping by the wedding guests.

The End.

Printed in Canada